"*Less is More* is a rare blessing of a book – simple, profound, and practical. Brian Draper takes you gently along the path less travelled, to the place where the life you want can be found where it always was, in the life you have."

Loretta Minghella OBE, CEO Christian Aid

"When I first met Brian I was struck with what a clear voice he has for articulating faith in the modern world in a new way. I'm thrilled that he's continuing to give us books like this one. Prepare to be illuminated and inspired."

Rob Bell, bestselling author and speaker

"In the busyness of day-to-day existence – filled with frenetic distractions and diverting amusements – Brian Draper's writing inspires us to stop long enough to listen to the whisper of our souls, to rediscover the sacred wonder of life, and to celebrate our place in the world."

Steve Chalke MBE, Founder of Oasis Global & Stop The Traffik

LESS IS
MORE

LESS IS
MORE

BRIAN DRAPER

LION

Published by Lion Books
an imprint of
Lion Hudson plc
Wilkinson House, Jordan Hill Road,
Oxford OX2 8DR, England
www.lionhudson.com/lion
ISBN 978 0 7459 5551 3 (print)
ISBN 978 0 7459 5864 4 (epub)
ISBN 978 0 7459 5863 7 (Kindle)

First edition 2012

Acknowledgments
Scripture quotations taken from
the Holy Bible, New International
Version, copyright © 1973, 1978, 1984
International Bible Society. Used by
permission of Hodder & Stoughton, a
member of the Hodder Headline Group.
All rights reserved. 'NIV' is a trademark
of International Bible Society. UK
trademark number 1448790.

pp. 57, 67 scripture taken from The
Message. Copyright © by Eugene H.
Peterson1993, 1994, 1995, 1996, 2000,
2001, 2002. Used by permission of
NavPress Publishing Group.

pp. 37, 39: From *Simple Pleasures: Little
Things That Make Life Worth Living*
published by The Random House Group,
2010. Printed with permission of The
National Trust.

pp. 59–60: From *Deep Country: Five Years
in the Welsh Hills* by Neil Ansell (Penguin
Books, 2011). Copyright © Neil Ansell,
2011.

pp. 88–89: From "The Secret of Adele's
Success? No Festivals, Tweeting – Or
Selling Out" copyright © Adam Sherwin,
24 May 2011. Reprinted by permission
of the *Independent*.

pp. 97–98, 99: From *Born to Run* by
Christopher McDougall copyright ©
Christopher McDougall, 2010. Reprinted
by permission of Profile Books.

p. 114: From *A Time for New Dreams*
copyright © 2011 by Ben Okri. Reprinted
by permission of The Random House
Group and The Marsh Agency Ltd.

pp. 128, 131: From "Vegas" by Martyn
Joseph. Copyright © Martyn Joseph, 2007.

pp. 138–40: Excerpted from *The Hidden
Spirituality of Men: Ten Metaphors to
Awaken the Spiritual Masculine* © 2008 by
Matthew Fox. Printed with permission
of New World Library, Novato, CA.
www.newworldlibrary.com

p. 152: From the book *The Power of
Now* copyright © 1997 by Eckhart
Tolle. Reprinted with permission of
New World Library, Novato, CA. www.
newworldlibrary.com

p. 153: From "Mere Science Cannot
Account for Beauty" copyright ©
Michael McCarthy, 25 March 2011.
Reprinted by permission of the
Independent.

p. 156: *The Running Sky: A Birdwatching
Life* by Tim Dee, published by Jonathan
Cape. Reproduced from © Tim Dee,
2009 by permission of United Agents
Ltd and The Random House Group
Limited. (www.unitedagents.co.uk) on
behalf of Tim Dee.

p. 161: Copyright © Edward Esch, Latin
translation by Charles Anthony Silvestri.

Illustrations © 2012 Chantal Freeman
http://divaarts.com

A catalogue record for this book is
available from the British Library.

To Betsy-Joy.
You came, trailing clouds of glory.

"The less you have, the more you can give, and the more you have, the less you can give."

Mother Teresa

Contents

Introduction

There must be more to life than this. Mustn't there?

The feeling arrives, for me, late at night, when I cannot sleep; or after I have read another article about the destruction of the rain forests; or when I have chatted to comfortably off, polite, and ordinary people who are burned out and at their wits' end; or after I have walked past another homeless person; or wasted another evening watching mindless TV.

There must be *so* much more.

The trouble is, we are in an awful bind. For even when we sense this deeper desire for something qualitatively "more", our programmed response is to go out and increase quantity – by earning more, buying more, having more, achieving more, and always trying to become more along the way...

And we do this because we struggle to imagine how life could be any different.

But what if the universe wasn't set up this way, for us to keep taking more and making more for ourselves? Have you ever noticed, in fact, how, when we try to get more, we seem to end up with less? With less peace, less time, less wonder, less *life*?

It's strange, but it's like there's a law at work.

What if the universe instead is a counter-intuitive place in which you gain more by having less, in which you achieve more by striving less?

Imagine – in this upside-down (or is it right-way-up?) world – if you were able to go further in this life by stopping, if you could get there quicker by slowing down; imagine if you could acquire so much more by learning to let go of everything you think is *yours*!

On paper it seems like madness but – and this is the magical thing – it begins to make sense when you dare to try it for yourself. In fact, it *only* makes sense when you try it for yourself...

I don't know about you, but I desperately want to start living fully before I die (no matter what I believe about the afterlife), and I am ready to try anything, however counter-intuitive.

I want to become part of the solution, not the problem, in *this* life. I want to look my children in the eye and say:

I played my part. I woke up.

I came back to life.

How to Use This Book

So I started wondering:

> How can we disrupt our deadening routines?

> What will it take for us to ditch "life as we know it" in pursuit of something better?

> How can we loosen our grip on what we possess (and what possesses us)?

> How can we make space to breathe – to live?!

> How can we become more *present* when we are so distracted?

> What do we really want to do with our life?

> How can we tune in to the Spirit of life, the force for good in this world?

> How can we make the difference that *we alone* were put on Earth to make?

The reflections that follow – which form a loose pattern – explore some of these questions and themes. To experience real transformation (which is what I hope to achieve in my own life) you can't start with bald facts, lifeless propositions, established "truths". In fact, we need to unlearn so much! So we start, here, with metaphor: playful, exploratory images and symbols that may help us to burst out of our narrow imaginations and strait-jacketed lives and dream something simpler, more sustainable – *spiritual* – for life in this busy world.

Please take it slowly. Chew. Ponder. Dream. Inhabit the metaphors. Apply the stories. Listen to your soul.

I've gathered some bullet points as I go, into a "manifesto". It's for my sake, as I tend to forget so easily; but I hope it helps you to reflect on how your life can also change – for good.

The guiding principle, should we dare to apply it, is simple: that *less*, somehow, is *more*. Life is not about quantity, but quality.

We have a choice, then. Carry on regardless, business-as-usual, and sink into resignation; or feel for the awakening of our soul and for the guiding of the Spirit of life (which personally I take to be God). As soul and Spirit meet, we find a way forward.

There must be more to life than this, after all...

So much more.

Brian Draper

Prelude: The Snow

Snow is falling. Outside, cars are skidding up
the hill, and then back down again. Wheels
are spinning but they're going nowhere fast.
The trains have stopped. The groceries can't be
delivered. School's out. A thousand best-laid plans
have been put on ice – for today, at least.

And these gifts of disruption are priceless.

Not just because (in this case) we get to go
sledging instead of slogging it into work, or
because the landscape goes so beautifully white
before our eyes. No, these gifts of disruption are *so*
precious because they stop us in our tracks.

"Stop what you are doing and listen," they seem
to say.

When was the last time you did that?

Listen: not just to the silence of the snowfall,
which muffles so much noise on the outside. But
listen to the sounds *within* you, too: to the inward
groans of frustration and sighs of annoyance
which arise the moment we are held up, in any
way; to the impatient drumming of fingers in our
head if the lights turn from green to red when we
have somewhere to get to, fast.

It takes time to stop. If you're speeding in a
car and have to brake suddenly, momentum still
carries you forward – into your seat-belt, with
luck, and not through the windscreen. When

circumstances force us to stop, it's hard to halt the momentum *inside*. It takes a while to slow down, forget Plan A, and settle into the holy disruption of

what

might

now

emerge.

But if we *do* manage to settle, like the snow, then life can start to feel different.

Magical. Reconnected, somehow.

You might get less done. But there may be more – *much more* – to Plan B than you would ever have believed.

Less is More Manifesto:

I will pay closer attention to the disruptions and try to welcome them; I will look for what Plan B has to teach me.

QUEST,
QUALITY,
AND
QUESTIONS

1.

Leaving Home to Find a Home

It takes courage to make a new start – to try a new way of life, or find a different rhythm, or establish another way of being; but something within us – a more authentic voice than the superficial chattering of our ego-driven mind – quietly urges us to be brave, to go for it. If we heed that call of what we might call "soul", then we must be prepared to let go of life-as-we-know-it, and set out for the place where we most fully belong. We must leave home, in other words, to find our home again.

Homesick

There is no place like home, as the saying goes.

It's where you can know and be most fully known. Behind the scenes of your life, it's the place you return for sanctuary, warmth, food, love... And it's where you can offer hospitality, such a precious gift to bestow.

It's hardly surprising, then, that home has such an important place in our cultural and spiritual psyche. In many great stories the hero must leave home to undergo an epic, transformational journey. Frodo leaves the Shire. Dorothy leaves Kansas. Abram leaves Ur. Neo leaves the Matrix...

And it's a sickening feeling, stepping away from home, perhaps for the first time.

* * *

As children, home is the only place we know. When I was seven, I was invited to stay overnight with my cousin. He was my best friend, and lived only half a mile down the road. My parents dropped me off, but within half an hour they had to pick me up again, because I was so homesick.

Home is base camp, the centre of our universe. But even early in our lives, in our childhood, we must begin taking small steps away from it.

The first day of school is one such moment, a huge threshold to cross in our shiny new shoes, if we did but know it at the time. We cross others, too. The first time we step out of the front door to go to the corner shop on our own. The first time we are allowed to take the bus to the next town or village with a friend. The photograph we pose for, by the front door, of our first day at secondary school. The first party we go to that lasts late into the evening. The first time we bring a girlfriend or boyfriend home to meet the parents. The first time we sit behind the wheel of a car and learn to drive…

All are steps in the process of leaving. And then, one day, it comes. You walk away completely. Part of you feels like you are off on a great journey, never to look back; and part of you weeps inside like a seven-year-old who needs to be picked up early from a first sleep-over.

* * *

We must, at some point, leave home, to begin the great journey of *finding* our home again. We may have no idea what will happen along the way, nor even where we will end up making our home. All we know, instinctively, is that leaving home involves more than just leaving our parents behind and getting a place of our own.

It's about finding space in which to live and breathe; one writer, Richard Rohr, calls it "a metaphor for the soul". Home speaks to us, then, of deeper things.

I am looking to find not just a place to live, but a place *in the world*, and beyond that, a place in this universe. We are all looking, if we are honest, for a path home to the very heart of life itself.

To life as it was meant to be lived.

No wonder, deep down, we can all feel homesick, even if we're lucky enough to live in the nicest house that money can buy.

One Day, One Day, One Day

Setting out is such a powerful, dangerous, and inspiring thing to do.

The trouble is, usually when we find a *physical* place to call our own, we put the journey of our soul straight back on hold, almost before it has a chance to begin – while something a little closer to an ego-trip begins: filling and furnishing a house, storing and hoarding, improving and extending, and trying to maintain the whole lot. Any soulful sense of "departure" can soon be replaced with a false sense of arrival: of having made it and wanting to make some more.

Every now and again, of course, our soul will resurface to remind us that there must be more to life than this: when we lie awake at night; when we have a health scare; when we reach a milestone birthday; when a friend dies suddenly.

And when the soul stirs we promise ourselves that one day we *will* see the world, we *will* give something back, we *will* do what we dreamed of doing as a child, we *will* learn an instrument or climb a mountain, we *will* spend more time with our kids or our friends, we *will* find our true path, and that one day life *will* begin in earnest...

But first, our ego retorts, I must establish my place in life, get myself sorted, secure my reputation, earn a good salary, please my boss, prove my worth. Then I can do the rest...

How many of us say, "One day, I will retire, and do what I *really* want to do..." And how often do people fall ill, or become frail, or worse, before they have a chance to do all the things they'd been promising themselves for the better part of their lives? We delay our unique, authentic life while we save up to buy a manufactured one off the shelf.

There will always be a part of the outer wall of our life that needs work – the mock-Tudor beams will need painting, or the kitchen extending – before, it seems, we are willing to leave the personal castles we have built for ourselves and set back out on that soulful journey towards home.

No matter.

It is *never* too late to do so, if we are brave enough. The invitation to make the journey is always before us. We know it, deep down. When we stop, we can feel it, tugging away at us gently. The path stretches in front of us. All we have to do is to make that step back into the unknown again.

2.

Seeking Direction

A friend of mine used to command ships in the Royal Navy. He explained to me one day the difference between using a compass and gyroscope. It's a tantalizing metaphor, as we wonder what on earth can guide us – in such distracting, busy, selfish times – towards a simpler, sustainable, and spiritual life.

The Compass and the Gyroscope

A compass points you to an approximation of north – "magnetic" north. But on a ship there is so much metal that a compass reading can easily be distorted. It is vulnerable to interference. And if it's "out" by only a matter of degrees, it will lead you on the wrong course altogether.

A gyroscope, on the other hand, is an instrument that refers you to "true" north, and is not subject to the magnetic fields that can scramble a compass. It will point you in the right direction, no matter what the circumstances, no matter how choppy the seas, no matter what interference surrounds it.

* * *

When we try to navigate life with the equivalent of the compass – using our rational minds alone – we find ourselves subject to interference. Even if it points us in roughly the right direction, to magnetic north, the signal is frequently scrambled.

In particular, the commentary in our head, the inner monologue of our brittle ego, skews our sense of direction, through a mixture of fear, guilt, insecurity, and false expectations (usually the false expectations of others)...

From the moment we sit exams at school, or we're told we're good at this, bad at that, or different from the rest... from the moment we spot that friends have better toys, or their parents have a bigger house... from the moment we're told we're good for nothing (or better than all the rest)... from the moment we realize we can get a laugh by playing the fool, or win adulation by coming first... From that moment, our direction in life is compromised by the ego.

The consumerist world of "more, bigger, faster" compounds this interference. It declares that life is a competition and dares us to enter. It claims that the more you have, the better you are – and the better you are, the more you should have. It says it wouldn't be seen dead with that old phone, so upgrade it, *now*. It says, get the biggest mortgage you can, stretch yourself to the limit and maximize your returns... It says, look busy, lunch is for wimps, fill your boots, get ahead of the pack.

And between the ego and the consumerist world, the compass of our mind twitches and jags, and we are drawn off course.

* * *

But here's the good news.

The "compass" is not the only way to navigate a path through challenging times.

Our instinct tells us as much. The great artists sense and see and express it. Religions preach it, however clumsily. Children demonstrate it. We have moments of clarity which confirm it, fleeting glimpses of a truer sense of direction.

While, on the surface, the push of ego is strong, nevertheless, deeper below, we can detect the gentle, persistent nudge of *soul*. And while the "more, bigger, faster" consumer world appeals to our ego dramatically, explicitly, and seductively, there is something else calling to us, more winsomely, if we were to stop to notice: a Spirit – the Spirit of life, if you like – that whispers to us of a counter-intuitive world and of a different path to get us there.

The *alignment* between our own soul and this Spirit is like the ship's gyroscope. It steers us towards true north.

Why is it, then, that the gyroscope – that precision instrument of inner guidance – for most remains undiscovered?

* * *

The divine call and response – between soul and Spirit – is at work in us at all times, if we could simply become aware of it. Usually, the radio or TV is up too loud for us to notice. But even when we do stop to notice, we tend to fear this unfamiliar leading, which would steer us into uncharted territory – into places of stillness and silence, for example – and so we ignore it. It is, after all, a brave person who dares to divert from life-as-we-know-it, however stultifying that life has become.

Nevertheless, the soul will not compromise. It does not seek its identity in material possessions as the ego does, nor does it require us to finish first and get all the glory in life.

Instead, it has greater ambitions for us altogether: to help us find the gift we have been given in life – a gift unique to us, which cannot be earned or won, by definition! – and to offer this gift back in service to those around us.

If we really believe that "there must be more to life than this", then we must learn to notice when the soul stirs in us. And when the Spirit of life catches our attention – through things we hear, or see, or taste, or touch, or smell – then we should feel for where it leads.

For this alignment between soul and Spirit will take us towards the very heart of life itself, if we follow. It will start to lead us *home*.

Less is More Manifesto:

I will notice the way my ego pushes me, and the world of "more, bigger, faster" pulls me, in a direction that is not helpful. I will begin to notice the "call and response" below the surface of my life, between soul and Spirit, and try to let it guide me more.

3.

Possession

If we are to try to break a pattern and live differently – soulfully – then we need to examine our relationship to the things we own. Do we possess them, or do they possess us? It is time to loosen our grip.

My, My, My

What do you miss most when you find yourself in pursuit of a "more, bigger, faster" life?

The space to stop and draw breath?

The perspective to discern what really matters?

The openness to expect the unexpected?

The grace to receive from others?

The depth of closer relationships?

The freedom to be yourself?

The time to do the things that bring you alive?

We can miss so much... but most significantly, we can – very simply – miss the *point*.

And the point is this: that life is to be spent, not bought or earned or hoarded. It is a gift, of infinite worth, with which we have been entrusted, and which we can pass on to others.

We are already rich, in ways we have not realized or may simply have forgotten.

* * *

So how do you wish to spend your life?

Always on the run?

Constantly dissatisfied?

Forever wanting more?

Of course not.

It's just not worth it. Think of that sense of anticlimax when we treat ourselves to something new. As soon as we have it in our hands, psychologically it begins to feel out of date. It's strange: it may have been tempting us for months; we may have been dreaming of the day when it became ours. Yet its mesmerizing power now slips through our fingers. It drains. And as it does, we set our eyes on the next thing to pursue and possess once more...

Consumerism has a built-in obsolescence, for a very good reason: if we were *truly* satisfied with what we had, we wouldn't feel the urge to consume more and more.

It wears us out. And deep down, if we're honest, most of us are tired of being caught in such an endless cycle. We want to be liberated and reconnected with what it means to be human.

What more do you need, in order to become more you?

Nothing, of course.

* * *

One way to respond is to examine our relationship to the world of things – in particular, as the spiritual writer Eckhart Tolle suggests, to "things that are designated with the word 'my'... "

He tells the story of a woman he used to visit, who was riddled with cancer. She had months to live and was facing death with increasing serenity. But once, when he called to visit, the lady was unusually distressed; a diamond ring of hers had gone missing and she suspected that her housekeeper had stolen it.

Tolle asked her four simple questions about the way she was feeling, which helped her through. Each question was followed by a pause.

Do you realize you will have to let go of it at some point, perhaps quite soon?

How much more time do you need before you will be willing to let it go?

Will you become less when you let go of it?

Has "who you are" been diminished by this loss?

As her condition worsened, she decided, in response to Tolle's questions, to give more and more away, including – graciously – to the housekeeper. She experienced more joy as she did so, as she realized that she was not defined by anything she owned. (Happily, after she died, her ring was discovered among her things; it had *not* been stolen by the housekeeper, after all...)

* * *

If you like, you can invert Tolle's third and fourth questions, to ask yourself:

Will you become *more*, as a result of holding on to as much as possible?

Is "who you are" *augmented* by what you own?

If the answer to these questions is no, then your grip on the things you call "my" will have loosened, albeit for a moment – like a limpet that's sitting loosely on a rock. It's in these moments that we have the chance to act, to move the limpet, before it responds by sticking even more tightly.

The Spitfire

Think of it another way. Ask yourself: what would you save if you woke up in the night to find your house burning down?

You will probably surprise yourself pleasantly.

We often take the people in our life for granted, and neglect them as we work for the trappings of success. Yet wouldn't we instinctively try to save *people* from a fire, because we know deep down what truly matters? When it's a matter of life or death, our perspective shifts, usually for the better, as it did for the lady with the ring.

After people, you can probably think of one or perhaps two things that have great sentimental value: a book, or a photo album, or a keepsake. It's funny, when you stop to think, but you probably wouldn't be desperate to save the biggest or most expensive things first. There are other, humbler items of much higher worth.

One of my most precious possessions is a small piece of copper given to me by my grandfather. It has no material value – it used to be an old penny, in fact, and was whittled into the shape of a Spitfire by a German prisoner of war during the Second World War. The prisoner gave it to my grandfather as an act of friendship and reconciliation. And so its intrinsic worth grew.

Grandpa then passed it on to me, when I was really quite little. What made him trust me with it? I have no idea, but that makes it more precious still. I can imagine the first time it fell into my grandfather's (now long-gone) hands, and here it is, now, in mine.

So if *most* of my possessions are ephemeral, why do I want more of them? Nothing can get more precious than the Spitfire I'm looking at here, as I write, along with some of my children's artwork, and a few notebooks, letters, and photos. A handful of hand-me-downs for the next generation, which no amount of money could ever buy.

* * *

One way of acting as we momentarily loosen our grip on all that we have, is to begin giving things away, like the lady in Eckhart Tolle's story. A friend of mine has decided to give one thing she owns away every day, in a brave attempt to reassess her relationship to her things, and to ensure that she travels more lightly through the rest of her life.

You might like to try something similar, even if it's to think about just one thing you could donate. It would be more powerful if you cherish the object; I imagine it was a wrench for my grandfather to give me the Spitfire, looking back. But his "less" became so much more within me.

The Bottle of Water
The best things in life are free. It's a cliché, of course, but it's true.

Look at advertisements. Long ago they stopped focusing on the functions of a product itself – how much better it performs than its rivals, or what sets it apart technically, or how much it costs, or what it does...

That's because advertisers understand keenly that it's not products themselves which are desirable within a crowded market, but the emotional or spiritual associations we make with them. These associations are made credible through a powerful narrative, inspiring imagery, poetic wordplay, and repeated airings on the TV or the billboards.

How many myths have we bought into? How much stuff have we come to desire which we had no real desire for in the first place?

* * *

Bottled water is a classic, perhaps *the* consumer icon of our times. In recent years, the bottled water industry has grown huge, but this was only after companies such as Evian and Perrier wove sophistication into their branding, and people bought into it. Ever since we have witnessed a proliferation of companies all selling the same thing in variously labelled bottles.

It falls from the sky, and (after we have paid our water bill) it flows freely from our taps. Yet still we choose willingly to pay extra for it to come in a bottle (£25 a go, for some "exclusive" ranges).

Of course, we are not just buying water. Perhaps we are buying convenience, if we are out and about. But, beyond that, we have a natural thirst for something deeper and purer in life, which refreshes us in a way that goes beyond the physical. We have an emotional and spiritual thirst, which we try to slake by buying into the *idea* of drinking spring water.

We've become so used to the idea of buying water now that this seems normal – despite having it freely on tap, and despite all the extra energy and oil required to make so many millions of plastic bottles. Even more absurdly, TV commercials for bottled water may appear alongside news of droughts and water shortages in developing countries.

* * *

It's not just bottled water that carries an emotional or spiritual attachment, of course. The "sports utility vehicle", we hope, may give us a whiff of purposeful adventure, and make us feel like a trail-blazer, a pioneer perhaps, even as we sit in the traffic jams of the daily commute or suburban school run. We hope the beauty products we buy "because you're worth it" will make us feel like we are indeed worth that much more – as if make-up or anti-ageing cream or shampoo could *honestly* add a single jot of value to you, as a person.

(How much *do* you think you are worth, by the way?)

It's the promise of an emotional and spiritual reward that persuades us to part with cash for products we might otherwise not dream of buying – because our culture sells back to us what was free from the start: the very best things in life.

Adventure

Purity

Identity

Freedom

Joy

Wisdom

Companionship

Courage

Inspiration

Artistry

Uniqueness

Daring

Laughter

Creativity

Love

Who on earth gave permission for anyone to take those amazing ingredients of life, package them up, and sell them back to us for a profit?

(Answer: we did.)

The good news is that you don't *have* to buy back what is already yours. Ego will push us to invest our worth in what's supposedly even better than the real thing; meanwhile, soul and Spirit will always point us, if we are willing, towards what is already ours, for free.

Life is Quality

When we think of our "quality of life", we tend to measure it in terms of luxuries. It has become a means of judging how far we have come in life. How many bedrooms does our house have? Can we afford a cleaner? Where do we go on holiday?

But there's a different "quality" to life altogether, waiting to be rediscovered.

It's quality when we make time to listen to how someone's day has been.

It's quality when we put others' needs before our own.

It's quality when we read to a child at bedtime without checking our phone for texts.

It's quality when we invite our neighbours around for a meal.

Some of these things may not be easy. But they yield a quality of life that is different from the norm. We know it, deep down.

The Simplest Pleasures

"The deepest pleasures almost always come from the simplest sources," writes Fiona Reynolds, the director-general of the National Trust in the UK, in her foreword to a book called *Simple Pleasures*. "It is one of the great delusions of our age that we can only find pleasure in ultra-sophisticated, expensive or complex situations... It is so often found in little, usually unremarked things and the cherished places in our lives that evoke comfort, joy and memories... Simple pleasures," concludes Reynolds, "are a vital ingredient in the important business of valuing what we have, not regretting what we have not." And she is absolutely right, of course.

A glance through the short contributions to Reynolds' book, made by different people in public life, provides a meditation in itself on what matters most:

A hot bath

Live music

Knitting

A log fire

Walking the dog

Chasing butterflies

Listening to owls at night

Running in the rain

Rambling

Litter-picking

Foraging for mushrooms

Painting the landscape

Working with wood

Gazing through a window

Bread and cheese

Morning sunshine

Baking with children

Reading

Finding solitude

We could add our own. I took enormous pleasure from clearing a corner of the garden recently. It was back-breaking work, and I did it all on my own. But I befriended a robin and a wasp, and found a rhythm to the work, making a connection with wood and earth and creature and leaf and life.

Sue Crewe – the editor of the magazine *House and Garden* – has a delightful "simple pleasure". Hers is to keep a "gratitude diary". The idea is to record five things every day that she is grateful for – written simply, without embellishment. She has done this religiously for many years, and while she would say it doesn't make for an especially thrilling diary, it does help her to keep things in perspective.

It provides her with a list of the things from each day that she was grateful for. And the gratitude itself, she believes, is what is transformative: "it takes up so much room that everything corrosive and depressing is squeezed to the margins."

"It seems," she decides, "to push out resentment, fear, envy, self-pity... leaving room for serenity, contentment and optimism to take up residence."

Simple.

Less is More Manifesto:

I will stop buying things for the sake of it, and look instead for where the best things in life are free at the point of need. In the meantime, I will examine the things that I call "my" own, and will start to give things away, at a pace I can sustain. I will improve my quality of life without trying to buy it.

4.

The Ordinary Day

We tend to seek fulfilment in the outstanding,
or exciting, or remarkable moments of life.
However, life itself is the outstanding, exciting, and
remarkable thing. And when we realize that, every
day becomes a gift to be relished.

Dull News Days

When we watch the news, it's easy to think it's boring if nothing sensational has happened. But isn't that a good thing?

I remember reflecting on how dull the turn of the millennium had been; how it seemed as though it promised so much, yet delivered so little. It was unspectacular, an anticlimax. It just ticked over.

And then 11 September 2001 happened, and the new century started with its dreadful bang. Much of the world woke up to the fact that the very ordinariness of a normal, sunny Manhattan morning in autumn had been something to treasure all along. It was a world to which we could never quite return.

So next time there is a dull news day, we should not forget to give thanks.

* * *

The unexpected diagnosis of a terminal disease; a sudden bereavement; redundancy; the words "it's over" spoken by the love of your life: at times like these, you would do anything – *anything* – just to bring your dull days back to life.

The Sunflower

In 2010, the British media reported the story of Kate Greene, who died from cancer, having been first diagnosed in 2008.

One night, she awoke at around 4 a.m., fearing that she wouldn't make it through until daybreak, and so she asked her husband urgently to fetch her a pen and paper, and began to write down her thoughts. She compiled what turned out to be a list for her husband and two young boys of a hundred simple points of common sense, advice, principle, and wonder.

> "Always kiss the boys goodbye and goodnight," she wrote.

> "Teach them to be on time, and to mean what they say."

> "Get a dining-room table and try to eat together."

> "Teach them to respect women, and never double date."

> "Never leave more than a week before making up – life is too short."

In the face of her own mortality, Mrs Greene drew deeply – and her searing clarity makes you ask whether life must really be so complex after all. She distilled the essence of what she loved to do, and what she wished she could have done, for the sake of her children. "Mummy," she wrote, "would have loved to have hand-fed a wild robin, like she used to feed the squirrels."

Quality.

For most of us, we hope, there is still time for such inspiring things. Her list certainly makes you wonder – and wondering is good for the soul, as any contemplative will tell you.

"Grow a sunflower now and again," she wrote. I think this is my favourite, for its simplicity and creativity and boldness. There is something about a sunflower, isn't there?

For your interest, the best time to grow one is after the last frost in spring. So why not put a note in your diary, as a fitting memorial both to this wise woman and to her idea, to engage in a creative act that could help us to search ourselves and to ask what truly matters, in the end.

* * *

If you were to write a simple list of common sense, advice, principle, and wonder, like Kate Greene did, what would be on it? And for whom would you write it?

Imagine someone reading it after you've gone. What would it tell that person about who you were and what you really valued in life?

How would it help to inspire them to live more vividly and simply?

Less is More Manifesto:

I will grow a sunflower, to remind me of the simple wisdom that will flow, if I let it, from deep within.

5.

The Appreciation Society

If we spend life comparing ourselves with others, we usually find ourselves wanting. But what would happen if we began to notice more of what we have than what we want? Aren't we, in fact, already rich beyond compare?

I Have Breath

"Think, for a moment, about a day in which we wake and remember what we already have, the blessings that we have already been given, the things that we have already earned, the love that we have already found," writes Andrew Bienkowski, a Polish psychologist who, as a five-year-old, was exiled to Siberia with his family, and who knows the meaning of suffering more vividly than we would care to imagine.

He started life by losing even the little he had, including his grandfather, who starved himself to death so that his grandson could eat his meagre rations. Thankfully, the grandson survived and learnt some powerful lessons.

We are prone, he observes, to focus on our "wants" instead of our "haves". But we could, alternatively, approach our present situation thinking this:

"I have breath!"

"I have life!"

"I have shelter!"

"I am *here...*"

Imagine starting each new day by saying this a few times over, before the worries and the fears rush in. Breath, life, shelter, presence – perhaps the greatest gifts we could receive, and yet the very things we are most likely to take for granted.

And here's a thought...

"If you are in a position to take things for granted," writes Bienkowski, "you are already blessed beyond your needs."

Another Way of Looking at It

I was walking my children to school one day, but my son was worried about going in. Not for any specific reason; he simply had a nagging concern about the way the day would unfold. (Don't we all, very often?) And so I asked a question, instinctively, almost out of the blue:

"What could go right today?"

It surprised us all, in a way, because it's not a question we usually ask of each other.

Even as I sit here, in a coffee shop, writing, the man who's having a business meeting at a nearby table has just announced, very loudly, in a deeply resigned voice, to his colleague, "What *can* go wrong, *will* go wrong." We look for it. We expect it.

But this time, on the school run, we thought counter-intuitively:

about the games he might play with his friends;

about what he might discover in class;

about how we could all expect the unexpected, in a good way.

He went in happy. And afterwards, I began to think about what might go right for me, too. It's catching...

When you stop to think about it, why *not* consider what could go right? For, when you do, you start to look with greater expectation for what will go well, instead of what will go wrong. And the good becomes easier to identify, and to celebrate, when it touches your life and you pass it on.

At the end of the day, it's also helpful to ask the complementary question, "Where did it all go right?" Try it. The list could be longer than you realize.

We usually tend *not* to take this line of enquiry because most humans are problem-solvers, who tend to look for things to fix, for what needs attention.

But when, exactly, did life become just another problem to be solved? Who said it was something to be fixed?

What if it were, instead, something rare to be witnessed, to be savoured, and to be appreciated?

The Everlasting Beginner

Such a positive way of looking – for what could go well, or what went right – has a name: "appreciative inquiry" (AI). It was coined by the leadership expert David Cooperrider, who says that AI is "a positive approach to change that focuses on a person (or organisation's) best attributes and practices."

But this isn't just for business or organizations. It's for life.

And we can become more effective in our *lives*, he suggests, the longer we keep what he calls the "spirit of inquiry of the everlasting beginner."

It's a lovely phrase, and while it may sound naïve, too often we try to act clever, for fear of looking stupid; or else we avoid taking risks when faced with a new challenge, sticking only to what we know from experience.

Appreciative inquiry is about saying "less is more": suspend your preconceptions and expectations for a moment and try to approach each new situation with the curiosity of a child.

* * *

Have you noticed how children are not afraid of asking "stupid" questions? When she was six, my daughter asked me if you could slide down rainbows. I wish I still had such capacity for foolish wonder.

* * *

It takes courage to ask the simple questions that everyone else is too afraid to ask. Remember the tale of the emperor's new clothes? The two weavers told the emperor – fearing they would lose their privileged status as imperial clothiers – that his new clothes would be invisible only to those who were incompetent or stupid. So no one spoke up, for fear of being branded incompetent. It took a child to ask if the emperor was wearing anything at all.

We should never take it for granted that we know, and we should never feel too afraid to ask: How can I do this better? How does this work? What difference can we make?

The most powerful way to make a difference, says David Cooperrider, "is to craft, and seed, in better and more catalytic ways, the unconditional, positive question."

* * *

When we compare ourselves with others, we tend to focus on the gap between us – whether it's a gap in talent, or resources, or looks, or status – which highlights what we're not doing as well as someone else, or what we don't have in relation to the other person, or what we're bad at.

It takes up so much of our energy, just trying to narrow the gap. But the point of life is not to become as good as, if not better than, someone else. It's to do what we've been put on earth to do, to the very best of our ability, in the way that only we can do it.

And nobody does *that* better than you.

* * *

The golfer Tiger Woods was never great at bunker shots. So he had a choice: spend lots of his time and energy trying to improve his shots from the sand, or – and this is what he chose to do – improve what he was best at, his drives and fairway shots, which would keep him out of the bunker in the first place.

How much of your time and energy do you spend trying to plan for all eventualities, or working on things you're not very good at? And how *could* you become even better at the things you have been uniquely gifted with, which, after all, are the gifts that will help you to make a difference, and to change the world around you?

It's a question – an unconditionally positive one, I like to think – that is worth asking.

Less is More Manifesto:

At the start of each day, I will remember this: I have breath, I have life, I have shelter, I am here. I will ask myself what can go right. At the end of each day, I will ask what did go right, and be thankful for it. I will focus less on the gap between me and my "competitors" and instead work on honing my own unique gift. And instead of looking jealously at others, I will encourage them to make use of their own gifts.

SILENCE, SPACE, AND SETTLING

1.

Being Present

When we become more alert, awake, and "present"
to the possibilities contained within one simple day
we also become more fully alive. Silence and stillness
are a necessary gateway into such "presence" – and
into a way of life in which the active pursuit of
less yields more than we might imagine.

The Voice of Silence

How do we break the pattern, and go in search of real life? One way is simply to stop, to clear away distractions, and to start to listen much more carefully. Not to the cacophony of people telling you how to find true enlightenment – that is just another form of distraction – but to nothing at all, for a change.

Less is more, after all.

There are so many voices in our everyday life that it is almost impossible to listen to *nothing*, of course. But when you discover what lies beyond the noise, and settle into it, it comes as a great relief to know that the answers flow most freely when we stop striving, stop trying to earn our salvation or worth, and allow less truly to yield more.

It is a mystery that only makes sense when you try it.

Silence is like a hand that patiently reaches out to help. Tragically, few people ever seem to reach out in response. But that's sometimes all we can do.

* * *

Can you remember what silence sounds like?

Like the rustling of leaves?

Like the creaking of a house?

Like the chatter of the birds?

Like the folding of waves?

Like the whirr of a fridge?

Like the drone of a distant aircraft?

Like the expanding of time?

Like creation?

Like the stilling of a mind?

Like the stirring of a soul?

Like someone standing with you, listening too?

Like the pulsing of blood?

Like the beating of a heart?

Like the call of the Spirit.

In *A Book of Silence*, Sara Maitland writes that silence is not "an *absence* of sound, but the presence of something which is not sound."

* * *

The first challenge is to make the space to stop and listen.

The second is to hear the voice of the silence itself.

* * *

There is nothing to fear, however. Frequently, we run scared of the void. We leave the TV or radio on to drown out the voice of silence, worried about what its whisper will contain. For it's hard to trust silence if we have not befriended it.

Yet, at any given moment, we can seek it and we can find it, and we can offer silence the chance, finally, to speak for itself.

* * *

Listening to nothing can be more profitable than listening to everything. It's a richer experience, but it's also a *completely* different art.

The less noise we make, the more we tend to hear and the better we listen.

While the cacophony of our culture confines and constricts us, silence takes us beyond the usual limits, into a place of greater possibility: the possibility, for a start, of reconnecting with the Source of life, at that meeting point of soul and Spirit.

The prophet Elijah heard a "quiet whisper" in the silence after the earthquake, the wind, and the fire had passed by his cave. What chance do we give ourselves of hearing such a voice?

Do Not Be Afraid to Miss the Bus

It's hard to listen to silence without drifting away on a sea of thoughts. We find it almost impossible to sit still and be quiet, without our minds going into overdrive. And when they do, they drag us away from the present – taking us back into the past or forward into the future, but rarely, if ever, letting us settle in to "the now".

If silence is a friend we've turned into a stranger, then the present is like a land from which we have been exiled. Call it Eden, or the Promised Land; call it what you will, but the present is full of life. And it's always worth a visit.

* * *

Our fierce inner momentum pushes us constantly away from "here". The world of "more, bigger, faster" pulls us seductively over "there", where we think we will be better off. Our mind races and whirrs. But for our own sake, we have to stop trying to get somewhere else, fast. Otherwise we will forever be carried away by our thoughts and never learn to settle.

* * *

Imagine, for a moment, that each thought you have is like a bus that pulls up outside your house or office. You have two options: you can notice that the bus is there, run outside, jump aboard, and let it take you somewhere (anywhere!) far away from here.

Or you can notice that it's outside, but stay where you are and listen to it drive off into the distance, before all goes quiet again. Don't be afraid to miss the bus.

If we let the bus drive off instead of jumping on it, we give ourselves permission to remain a while longer in the present. And once we become a little more used to being there – *here, in fact* – then we find it's a place we can sink deeper into, a richer place entirely to explore.

* * *

Try it. Try sitting quietly and being still. *Nothing more.*

Once you've reached a point of stillness where you feel relaxed enough just to notice your thoughts, like the buses, coming and going, you'll be in a better position to listen to the stillness and silence that lie behind, and beyond, your thoughts.

And deep within the presence of that stillness and silence, as you linger there, listening, another voice beyond your mind speaks quietly, gently to you, of who you are and what you love and how you can touch the world through your own unique presence, just by being *here*.

As the Biblical proverb states, "Many words rush along like rivers in flood" – the flood of your mind – "but deep wisdom flows up from artesian springs."

* * *

The present is a soulful place. And it's a shame we rarely stop for more than a quick look around. A text comes in, an e-mail pops up, the phone rings, the TV blares, the radio crackles, someone tweets you and you're back to it. You're out of here, jumping on the bus.

But you don't have to. You really don't have to.

Stay a while. It may seem like a strange place to be, but it's the place that starts to lead us home.

Just William

I visited a monastery. And there, over a cup of tea and a slice of fruit cake, I started chatting to William, a Benedictine monk. "How long have you been here, William?" I asked, casually, as if he were an office temp or a barman.

"Thirty-nine years," he replied. "I arrived in 1970."

One of the vows a Benedictine monk makes, he told me, is "stability". And that means committing to a place, for life. The only way he plans to leave is "in a box", and even then it'll just be out of the back door and into the garden cemetery. But his most striking comment then followed: he gestured to the small lounge in which we were having our tea, and said, quite simply, with a smile:

"This is me."

* * *

There is great "presence" at that monastery, which is, surely, because the monks are simply "there": not straining into the future or looking back into the past, but settling, each day, into their well-worn habit of prayer and hospitality. Time is marked by the ringing of bells for each "office" throughout the day, when they gather to pray or read the psalms. But time, aside from that, seems somehow irrelevant. Things just are, and were, and will be.

Seeing William sitting there, intent on going nowhere slowly and carefully, made me wonder how much time we can kill if we're *not* careful – wishing something more exciting would unfold, or wishing it was the weekend, or wishing our meeting would finish, or wishing that the kids were in bed already, or wishing we were on holiday or that the train would hurry up and leave and

wishing,

wishing,

wishing our life away,

minute by minute, hour by hour.

What an unholy waste of time.

William has lived two-thirds of his days under the rule of St Benedict; and yet, as he tells me, "every day is different". Perhaps, if we can learn anything from his unhurried, rooted example, it is perseverance and presence; his quiet, seemingly insignificant "less" of a life, the heart-beating rhythm of an altogether more timeless truth.

Part of the Landscape

When he was thirty, Neil Ansell accepted the offer of living in a secluded cottage in mid-Wales. It was an experiment, for him, in "how lightly [he] could tread upon the Earth." (And he has written up the five years he spent there in a delightful book called *Deep Country*.)

"This was the pattern of my days," he writes: "a simple life led by natural rhythms rather than the requirements and expectations of others." He had no rent to pay, so wasn't beholden, as such – but neither did he have water, electricity, or gas, so it was no picnic in the park. (He had to work painfully hard to keep going, and shared his home with a colony of bats and a platoon of mice, except in the winter, when it was too cold for both bat and mouse.)

Before long, however, he noticed a strange thing. Instead of becoming more introspective as he'd expected, the reverse happened. He did not spend all his time thinking about himself, reflecting on his own life, raking over the past, and straining to pre-empt the future. Instead, he found himself settling in to the present, and moving his self out of the way, completely.

"My days were spent outside, immersed in nature, watching... My attention was constantly focused *away* from myself... And my nights were spent sitting in front of the log fire... staring at the flickering flames. I would not be thinking of the day just gone," he writes. "And I would not be planning tomorrow; tomorrow would take care of itself. The silence outside was reflected by a growing silence within. Any interior monologue quietened to a whisper, then faded away entirely..."

"I had become," he concludes, "a part of the landscape."

Fully present, then. Part of the scene, of *that* very day. Being who he was, within it. His relentless inner momentum had faded to nothing, without any pull from the disappearing world of "more, bigger, faster". Instead, the nudge of his soul and the call of the Spirit around him took him deep into the heart of stillness and assurance and oneness and peace.

Less can be huge, if we're serious.

Perhaps our own inner monologue pipes up in defence of the life we have chosen. *It's all right for someone like him! He's chosen to live in a secluded cottage in Wales. Where would we be if we all headed for the hills?* It's a fair point. We can't all do this. But it does seem as if the people who are most serious about disconnecting and reconnecting are also the ones who become most fully present, somehow, for whom life gains perspective.

They must have something to teach us about how we can live from day to day. And how we can play our part – however small – in becoming more present: a part of the landscape, on this very day, within *the* presence of the Spirit of life.

Time

What's the first thing you do when you wake up in the morning?

I think I know.

You look at the time. And for the rest of the day, unless you are blissfully distracted or on holiday, you live by the rule of the clock. And often you feel its pressure.

And yet, the funny thing is, we spend much, if not most, of our time "absent" from what lies before us. The clock is ticking, but we waste minutes every hour, and hours every day, living in the past or the future.

It's great to learn from the past, so long as it affects the present positively, and we don't *dwell* on it. And it's excellent (and essential) to set future goals, so long as we seek to meet them one step at a time within the present – and don't simply obsess about the time when we will achieve them.

There is so much to notice along the way, but if we look back constantly, or speed forward incessantly, the details become a blur: the flowers by the wayside, the colours of the sunset, the smell of the coffee.

The taste of life.

Less is More Manifesto:

I will spend a manageable period of quiet
during each day, when I will do nothing
but listen to the silence. I will learn
to befriend the silence and explore the
present. I will stop wishing my life away,
and settle in more fully to the unfolding
rhythms of each day. I will learn from the
past, and set goals for the future, but
will go one purposeful step at a time, from
now on.

2.

What Rents Your Space?

Taking our first steps into silence and stillness can be exhilarating, but also infuriating. Because when we pause, we can see, more clearly and perhaps for the first time, just what is going on in our minds. All the interference and distraction...

Our outer lives can be so crammed with junk and "stuff" - our houses, our lofts, our garages - that we just get used to living with it all. And that's an outward manifestation of an inner malaise. We are stuffed so full, mentally, emotionally, and spiritually, that it's hard to live with a lightness of being. The first step, then, towards transformation is simply to become aware of what's within us. The next is to make room for what matters most.

The Loft

Everyone knows it's wise to de-clutter our physical space from time to time. It can become overcrowded, and the space grows smaller and smaller. But how often do we de-clutter ourselves? Have you even thought about what *crowds* the space inside your head?

Let's do a quick inventory.

Think of the brand names, for a start. How many could you bring to mind in ten seconds? Speak them or write them down. You may be surprised at how many you come up with.

These brands have moved in on you, usually uninvited – a bit like the rat that moved into my loft this winter. They take up room, and mental capacity. And they vie for your attention; each makes a claim about itself and tries to make a claim upon you.

What about the soap stars, the film stars, and the pop stars? How many of those can you think of, off the top of your head? Imagine them all standing in a room, talking at the same time...

And how about the characters from your past that haunt you? A first boss who was a bully, or a teacher who said that you didn't have what it takes, or a parent who compared you unfavourably with your brother or sister.

What an unholy cacophony.

Who else or *what* else crowds your mind? Fears? The fear of being found out, perhaps. Or of being let down, or getting it wrong. Fears can spread quickly. They whisper more loudly than most of us can shout.

Our urgent, uncompleted tasks inhabit our minds, too, on a permanent basis, it seems. They drain our mental energy. You might complete one task, but two seem to arrive to take its place.

What are You Attached to?

And then there are the *attachments* we make to things in our mind, whether it's to what we own, or how we're perceived by others, or to things people have said or done to us...

We attach ourselves mentally to all kinds of things and hoard them in our mental lofts.

Such attachments probably take up more mental and emotional space than anything else. Perhaps someone has said something that you simply can't get out of your head; something that's stopping you from doing good work (they may have said that you're no good at a particular task) or from moving on emotionally. But you won't let go of this, consciously or not, because our minds like to hold on to wounds, and fashion a sense of identity from them.

It can be so hard to get rid of anything we pick up in life. But let go we must, in the end. You can't take anything with you into the next life, anyway – so it makes sense to learn how to travel lightly now, to let go, and to make space for what matters most.

Emptying the Trash

When we delete an e-mail, we don't, in fact, get rid of it. It simply goes into a "deleted e-mails" folder. We still need to empty that folder to finally clear any mail we no longer wish to keep. Otherwise the hard disk of the computer will still be filled with unwanted correspondence.

It's the same when you dump an unwanted computer file into "trash". You may have put it in the computer's bin, but you still have to *empty* that bin – otherwise no extra space will be freed up.

And as for computers, so for ourselves. It's one thing to bring something to mind that you would like to remove, and stick it in your "trash" – perhaps by grudgingly accepting that you need to let it go. It's another thing entirely to be willing to empty the trash and say goodbye to it forever. For that, we must be willing to clear permanently anything that's occupying space unhelpfully.

It's not easy. This is a lifelong task, which involves loosening our grip on the things we call "our" own, learning to untangle our sense of identity from our achievements, status, and belongings, and also learning how to forgive and to be forgiven. All we can do is to take small steps, perhaps, along this different path, into a world in which "love keeps no record of wrongs".

That's what Paul writes in the passage from the Bible (1 Corinthians 13:5) which is quoted at most marriages, Christian or not. It's perhaps one of the most challenging statements ever written. But if love keeps no record of wrongs, then isn't there more space in a life of love for better things, in the end?

* * *

Why not clear your loft, physically?

I have found that when you combine spiritual reflection with physical work, good things emerge.

* * *

Feed Your Mind

If you now have a little room for what really matters, then what *does* really matter? How do we feed our minds or, more pertinently, our souls, positively, as we try to find our way home, to the heart of life?

This is what Paul has to say elsewhere:

> *you'll do best by filling your minds and meditating on things true, noble, authentic, compelling, gracious – the best, not the worst; the beautiful, not the ugly; things to praise, not things to curse.*
> (Philippians 4:8)

It's sage advice. Somehow, we should try to open the shutters. Let some light in. Get the air circulating. It can get awfully dusty up there.

That doesn't mean we have to fill up our capacity again, once we have made room.

Quality time spent absorbing one poem, one piece of art, or one song will yield more food for the soul than a thousand web pages absent-mindedly surfed, or TV shows lethargically consumed.

The Object of My Focus

Even if we commit ourselves to spending more time reflecting on "things to praise, not things to curse", it's easy to become distracted. We can still end up mentally frazzled as we try simply to navigate our way through a day filled with words and images, tweets, texts, and e-mails.

In today's world, we suffer information overload. There are literally millions of avenues to explore at any given moment, just by going online. I typed "information overload" into my search engine, and 3,220,000 results were found within 0.12 seconds. That's what we're dealing with.

Contemplatives offer a helpful way to go in a culture that is just so bewildering (in fact, it feels as if they were made for such a time as this). They are good at *meditating* on one thing in particular – just one thing – and maintaining their mental, physical, emotional, and spiritual focus on it for a prolonged period. It's often (and especially) something very ordinary.

So they will observe an object closely – such as a candle flame, or a leaf, or a bird singing, or a river flowing – and keep watching, and watching, or listening, and listening... allowing their minds to become still in the process, empty of fidgety thoughts and full of attention instead.

And as they do so, they become slowly but vividly more present to the object and to themselves, and in the meantime the distractions fade away.

Anyone can practice this kind of contemplation – it's not just for spiritual or religious people – and, by doing so, we can learn how to become more focused and present to whatever it is that is put before us: whether it's a person who needs our attention, or a task at work, or a goal we've set in life...

In taking time out to do *less*, we can sharpen our focus for when it is time to act and, as a result, we may find ourselves achieving *more* in the process.

Less is More Manifesto:

I will de-clutter my mental space, keep fewer records of wrong, and spend more time letting the light into my mind from inspiring sources. I will practise contemplating "ordinary" objects, to slow myself down, and sharpen my focus within the present moment.

3.

How to Make Something Out of Nothing

Space – like silence and stillness – is a rare commodity in today's world. We crave space, to think, to breathe, to live. But how can we make space? Where can we find it? And what does it do to us when we find it and let it work its magic?

Outer Space

It's an awe-inspiring thing to stand on the edge of our small planet on a dark night and contemplate such a vast expanse of open space before and beyond us. Not that we do it very often; there's usually something on TV. But when we do, it can feel like staring into nothing, yet everything, at the same time.

We have made our home in space. Perhaps that's why it moves us, when finally we make some space for ourselves, too – space which is filled with nothing, yet everything...

* * *

The space is there to find, if you are willing to look.

Think of a cathedral. A monumental space created by human hands, many years ago. The space you now see inside as you walk though its great doors has been sculpted from nothing, as builders and craftsmen enfolded it with bricks and mortar, pillars and arches, windows and doors...

It's a contained space and, in a sense, it contains nothing, yet the emptiness is what charges it all with so much awe.

And sitting for a time within such nothingness is inspiring for the soul. We start to "inhabit" the space – and to feel connected, somehow, to generations' worth of humanity: not only to the people who shaped it in the first place, but to the throngs who have come in to pray, or to sing, or to mourn, or to celebrate, or to sit still, like us, just to be part of it all.

And the most liberating thing is, you don't need to fill such a space with *anything*. You don't need to talk. You don't need to busy yourself. You don't need to justify yourself within it. In fact, the space almost requires that you do the opposite.

Notice how most people speak in hushed, reverential tones. The space affects us. We may feel that we want to switch off the phone, settle in to something different, an other way of being, albeit for a little while.

And it's at that point – if we've slowed our inner momentum well enough – that somehow, mysteriously, we find ourselves at peace, *aligned*: we have become part of the space and the space has become part of us: settled.

Here you may find the space to think (and not think), space to listen, to gain perspective, to breathe, and to expand into the person you were created to become – into a being, and a way of being, that is so much more expansive than anything in your limited experience of life-as-we-know-it.

Sometimes I can try so hard to be "someone" that I don't give myself the space to be me.

Inside Out

Different spaces affect us in different ways, of course. Some are physically cavernous and inspire awe because of their size; others lift our hearts because of their quality of light, perhaps, or their atmosphere; still others may be profoundly simple, yet simply profound.

There is a tiny church above one of the ancient gateways to my home city of Winchester. It's nothing much more than a room, very plainly furnished, with small, simple windows. But it has stood there, set apart, for the last 750 years – this single, simple room, right above the archway.

You can step off the busy pavement, up its little steps, and into a place that, while only physically small, seems to be a gateway into another world – into an unchanging sense of "now" that carries you beyond the transitory and into the transcendent.

Step through such a gateway, and something in the space – the Spirit of life? – feels distinctly present, and calls to the soul.

It's like you're switching channel, from a world outside to this one here; a world that's *still* here, and has been all along. And so, here, you can sink into a time beyond time.

In the outside world, the space around us is shrinking with every passing week. There is always something more to fill it: cars, planes, music, meetings...

Here, though, space unfolds and we can find ourselves turned positively inside out.

And what we will find, if we spend time in such a space, is this: that there is more room on the inside of our life – far more – than we may have realized, and there is so much more to us than meets the eye.

* * *

Space has the capacity both to diminish and to expand us in equal measure. We are nothing but the tiniest, momentary speck within the vast nothingness of everything (and sitting in that little church above the gateway, we realize how many people have come and gone, been born and died, and that I shall be just one more passing through this gateway); yet wonderfully, simultaneously, it is *our* privilege – and our duty – consciously to experience this universe, while we are here.

To bear witness to it.

And we bear witness most fully when we cross the border from the outer to the inner world. We bear witness to a space that most are too busy to notice. In such a place as this simple room, which is free to enter – a place of less – I find myself standing on the threshold of something more beautiful than anything our world of "more, bigger, faster" can try to sell me.

Border Crossing

The ancient Celts cherished what they called "thin places", usually outdoor sites where it felt as though the gap between heaven and earth was somehow narrower – places where, for example, the sea met the shore, or mountains touched the sky. The Celts believed these places were thresholds, gateways to another world.

We tend to respond to such places instinctively, because our souls know that we need them, even if *we*, at a conscious level, do not. That's why we can feel that we're coming alive when we find them.

* * *

In thin places, we do not have to pretend to be someone we are not.

What is the point, after all, in pretending to the forest, or to the hills, or to the river, or to the sea, that you are someone other than who you really are? They know.

In this kind of place, roles mean nothing. Titles mean nothing. Status means nothing. While *you* mean everything.

You mean everything: especially because you are part of the place yourself, and you add your own grace and beauty to it, *without having to try*. The trees do not have to try, after all. The rivers do not have to try. Neither does the sea, the sky, or the birds. They simply are.

As you can simply be.

Within the thin spaces where heaven meets earth – and where, we might say, our soul meets the Spirit of life – it is possible to glimpse the person you were created to be.

* * *

Of course, you don't have to live by a mountain or the sea to find a place where your soul is stirred by the Spirit, or where heaven meets earth. It might be a favourite room you can return to every day where it's possible to be still, or a spot in your garden, or a bench at the allotment; it might be a view from a window in the city where you can simply stop and stare, or a green space, or a coffee shop with a good atmosphere.

There are threshold spaces everywhere when we start to look, border crossings to a world within our world: portals, gateways, entry points back to the path of the soul, to the journey home.

Less is More Manifesto:

I will look for gateways into the world of less is more, and I will deliberately step through them. I will practice lingering longer in soulful spaces, so that I can take this "spaciousness" back into the busyness of my everyday life, and let its quality be transformed.

4.

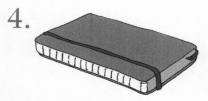

Mind the Gaps

When we rush headlong to achieve all of
our continually urgent tasks, it's easy to lose
perspective. Things can get on top of us. Life
feels out of control. However, something special
lies behind all the words, the activity, and the
noise: a blankness from which everything must
emerge and into which we all, in the end, will
return. I have begun to pay closer attention
to the white space between our words, to
the blanks in my diary, to the pauses in the
conversation. Without them, after all, everything
is Babel, and nothing makes sense that should
make sense.

"Let your words be few." (Ecclesiastes 5:2)

"He who holds his tongue is wise." (Proverbs 10:19)

The blank page can fill any writer with dread. I speak from personal experience of wondering where the words once sprang from and whether they will ever flow again. Such a fear results, usually, in one of two responses: we can freeze in terror, or spew words across the void until the void is no more.

Yet the blank page represents *such* promise! It is an invitation to make an utterance. It's an opportunity to express uniquely something of who you are, a chance to tell something of your story – but only when you are ready.

Without white space, there would be no meaning to the marks we make upon it. It's like the blankness out of which God said, "Let there be light." It's like the silence between notes that gives expression to music.

And while we're not all writers, in a way we are. It is unlikely that you will not send an e-mail or a text today. Each time you press "New Message", you are confronted with the blank page and this is your chance to use it well. It is an invitation to craft something from nothing, with care and with love.

And as for writing, so, too, for life: today itself is a blank page, offered.

We may, in our fear of blankness, already have scrawled meetings and appointments over this virgin day. Even so, try to notice the white space in between. Look for the gaps, for they may, in fact, contain the *real* clues to what this day holds. They may provide the space from which all of your other actions gain their meaning and their clarity.

Outside, a police siren rises from the silence and fades back into nothing again. Just as our very life emerges from nothing and fades back into nothing again when the time comes.

The Empty Diary

I wonder, what are the seemingly insignificant things that get squeezed out by the so-called important items in your schedule? The little things that actually mean more to you than you would prefer to admit to those who exert influence over your time.

Times, during the day, for a break, or for a little exercise, perhaps? (If you want to get fit, you have to start somewhere.) A cycle, twice a week, before work? A walk in the local woods at the weekend? A poetry evening or book club? A chance to talk to your spouse or partner?

Because the small, seemingly insignificant things in life can positively help to turn your life inside out, with a little attention and repetition. You don't always need to quit your job or travel the world to get your life back; you might simply start by making time to plant a sunflower.

* * *

"Your time is limited," said Steve Jobs, Apple's founder (who died in 2011), when he addressed students at a graduation ceremony at Stanford University. "Don't waste it living someone else's life…"

It's very easy for us to feel like victims. I have lost count of the number of times I've heard people (including myself) say, "There's nothing I can do to change things *at the moment* – my life is just too busy."

My life is too busy. To what end? For what purpose? For whose benefit?

* * *

The next time you are in a stationery shop, have a look at an empty diary, and ask yourself if you are a victim of life's busyness, or if you have simply victimized yourself.

If you were first to fill your diary with the small, insignificant things which usually get squeezed out, what would they be? Why do you let them get squeezed? And how would your life look if you managed to honour them?

The Pause in the Conversation

It's not just writers who are guilty of trying to fill space.

Ask yourself how you like to make conversation. Chances are, you'll hate with a passion those times when it all goes quiet and you can't think of anything to say, especially when you're chatting with someone you don't know so well. It *can* be awkward.

And yet.

Part of my work involves coaching people. And I don't mean standing on the touchline of a sports pitch shouting. Coaching, especially in the organizational sense, means asking open questions, speaking for little more than 20 per cent of the time, and listening like never before.

Sometimes, if I ask a really good question, the person I'm coaching will need *space* to sit and ponder, without feeling hurried or pressured to respond in a flash.

And if, as a coach, I then puncture the silence – afraid that the lack of talking is a sign the conversation is going badly – the chances are I will spoil the other's train of thought, lose the good work we have begun to achieve, and diminish the whole process.

* * *

Try asking someone a question, and then wait patiently for the answer, with curiosity and without hurry. Leave space for the person to answer. Show, by your body language and unhurried manner, that he or she has time to think before having to speak.

And *listen*.

If we allow the backdrop of silence to play its part, the quality of the person's answer and the quality of the time you spend with each other will increase dramatically.

The person you are listening to will not feel hurried, nor sense that he or she is about to be interrupted at any moment. You will both find an easier rhythm. And the space around the words will open up the scope of the conversation. This is a precious gift to offer anyone, and it is almost always rewarded with a compelling reply, one which will enrich you both.

We hear, and in turn, we shall be heard.

Less is More Manifesto:

I will learn to say more by using fewer words. And, in the meantime, I will listen more carefully to others. I will fill less diary time in advance, and think ahead about the seemingly insignificant moments of each day that I would like to regain.

RHYTHMS, RENEWAL, AND RECONNECTION

1.

Finding Your Rhythm

"Less is more" doesn't mean that we just while away our days doing nothing. It's about establishing a new balance and rhythm to life — one that will release us, in the end, to find a richer way of being, and to fulfil our potential. We may need to cut down on our busyness, but there are ways to do this that will help us achieve more, in the end, from less time and effort.

The Rhythm

Are you a machine? The way we live and work
these days, most of us seem to think we are (or
at least, should be). We act as if we can switch
ourselves on at the start of the day (with a strong
coffee), and proceed to multitask like a computer
until it's time to go home, late, for some snatched
conversations on the margins of life.

But the way we're working isn't working. At
least not according to the leadership expert Tony
Schwartz, in his book of that name. Schwartz
argues that we should remember how – and who
– we were created to be. (By inference, we have
forgotten.) We are "oscillatory" beings, he says,
not linear: we work in waves, rhythms, seasons,
and cycles. None of us can simply keep going.

As such, we should focus on how we manage
our *energy* more than anything else, he says, by
becoming aware of two things: how we *spend* our
personal energy and how we *renew* it. It's a very
simple way of thinking about life. (He subdivides
"energy" into four categories: physical, emotional,
mental, and spiritual.)

Intriguingly, we have "awake cycles", just like
sleep cycles, which last for about ninety minutes
before our energy dips. So Schwartz has created
positive rituals for himself to focus spending
his energy in what he calls "sprints" (during
these, he switches off the Internet and his phone
to avoid the constant little interruptions and
distractions that add hours on to our work each
day); after each "sprint" he changes focus entirely
in order to restore his energy – by going for a

walk or a run, or meditating, or reading, or by having a meal.

In this way, he says, he moves naturally between spending energy positively (in what he calls the "performance zone") and restoring his energy (in the "renewal zone"), and – crucially – he achieves more in less time.

This is the opposite of what many of us do, which is to keep slogging away, no matter what: oscillating instead between the "performance zone" and the "survival zone" – where we spend energy *negatively*. When our energy begins to dip, we reach for coffee or pills or chocolate, summon the adrenaline, grit our teeth, and try to hang in there.

After spending too long in the survival zone, however, it's all too easy to descend into a negatively passive zone called "burnout". In this "zone", we can end up trying to recharge our batteries by drinking too much, eating the wrong kind of comfort foods, zoning out in front of late-night TV, and getting fitful sleep when we finally go to bed, only to wake up feeling de-energized, instead of re-energized, as we could be – which is surely *not* how we'd like to live our lives, nor how we should lead others by example.

The good news is that we do not have to work *harder* to change our rhythm and regain the energy we so badly need. We can do more, with less.

Dare You Do Less?

In a recent interview with the highly successful British band the Arctic Monkeys, their lead singer, Alex Turner, was asked about his approach to music, life, and fame, and where his band could possibly go from "here"...

His answer was delightfully counter-intuitive:

"We want to get better rather than get bigger."

In the Zone

So how *do* we move seamlessly between performance and renewal during the course of a day? And how can we renew our energy positively, in a way that builds it back up ready for more action and helps us to achieve more in less time with a sharper focus?

Remember that our energy can be divided into four types: physical, emotional, mental, and spiritual. How can you actively renew or recharge each of these four types of energy?

Physical energy. The bedrock of all energy, Schwartz argues, is sleep. Most of us need seven to eight hours and, without it, we simply do not function as we could. With it, we have a foundation on which to build. During the day, you might have a walk, or take a nap (if it's possible), eat more healthily, drink plenty of water, change your scene at regular intervals... You don't need to stay in the renewal zone for ages, but you *must* do it properly when you go there!

Emotional energy. If you feel inspired, on top of things, and ready to go, you'll be drawing more deeply from inner resources, and your energy and enthusiasm will be infectious. Gratitude is an immense source of emotional energy, and the simple act of sending a note of thanks to someone, or making a note for yourself of things that have gone well, can help to renew and sustain you.

Mental energy is critical, and under constant threat in our culture of distraction. We need to give ourselves time to sink into one task well. But renewal is vital: your concentration will not last much longer than ninety minutes, at which point it is important to switch focus. This is where just a short period of stillness or meditation can be very useful, before you carry on.

Spiritual energy is what gathers everything else together. It's your reason for getting up in the morning, for keeping going through the day, and for looking after yourself carefully as you go.

Without a sense of purpose you will struggle to renew or to expend energy well. But *with* it, you will flow, and inspire yourself and those around you to work and play to a different rhythm – one in which you feel as good at the end of the day as you did at the start, having achieved more than you thought possible in less time and with less pain.

Staying Small when You Could Get Really Big

In the *Independent* newspaper Adam Sherwin described how one of Britain's most successful musical "exports" in recent years, the singer Adele, became hugely popular by "staying small".

"She refuses to headline Glastonbury, bans her hits from being used in advertising campaigns and won't turn her life into a soap opera," he writes.

According to Sherwin, Adele has a five-point plan for success:

1. She has no advertizing tie-ins. "I think it is shameful when you sell out," she says.

2. She restricts interviews and does not wish to be "ubiquitous".

3. She will not let her record company re-release her albums with a few extra tracks, tempting fans to buy the same thing over again.

4. She won't play the big festivals.

5. She won't play in big arenas, either, so as to maintain an intimacy with fans and to keep the spirit of her music.

The editor of Q magazine, Paul Rees, suggests that "A large amount of Adele's success is that she remains something of an enigma and we don't know everything about her... What has been lost in... [this] era is confidence in the idea that less is more."

Exactly.

Less is More Manifesto:

I will try to do more with less. I will notice the way I oscillate between spending and renewing energy, and keep a close eye on how long I spend in the performance, renewal, survival, and burnout zones. I will create small rituals to help me flow between performance and renewal, and create positive habits within the course of each day to help me recharge as I go.

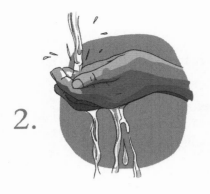

2.

Finding a Spiritual Source of Energy and Inspiration

It's our spiritual energy that helps to draw everything else together in life. But where do we go, ultimately, to find it? And how do we draw deeply from it?

The Well-Spring

Near to where I live, in Hampshire, there is an old house called Mottisfont, owned today by the National Trust. People come from all over the country (and the world, in fact) to see its celebrated walled rose garden, which is sublime in June.

The house is also lovely. Before it was handed to the National Trust it was a private and grand place, set in inspiring countryside. Yet originally Mottisfont was an abbey, and you can still see its spiritual foundations in its "cellarium" under the house. Monks had built a monastery on the site, establishing a community for a few hundred years before it was dissolved by Henry VIII during the English reformation.

The monks chose this spot because there is a well-spring. It is a gorgeous and gorgeously simple pool a couple of metres deep and a couple of metres wide. It looks as though the water is as still as a mirror. Yet a channel of water overflows from it constantly, and gathers pace as it heads downhill to become a fast-flowing, wide stream of clean spring water.

It's a place where you feel the nudge of your soul, and the call of the Spirit in almost equal measure.

In Saxon times, elders would summon their people from across the area to hold meetings (or "moots" as they were called) at the well ("font" – hence "Mottisfont"). It is awe-inspiring to stand quietly by this pool where, a thousand years ago, folk gathered together; it is a point of connection between humans and the earth.

The overflowing well became the principal source of water for a village that was built close by a few hundred years ago, for the monastery until it was dissolved, and then for the big private house.

And here's the amazing thing: over the course of the last thousand years the spring has never been known to run dry. This pool has drawn people to it, and they have, in turn, drawn from it, since as early as anyone can remember.

* * *

The Source

I once saw a little girl kneel instinctively beside the stream that flows from the well-spring at Mottisfont. She reached out her hand and cupped water to her mouth. She was drawn to it.

The nudge of soul is often more immediately apparent in a child.

But it made me wonder: From where can a child like her draw energy and inspiration as she grows up? What will sustain her, motivate, and inspire her? Where will she find refreshment for the journey ahead, away from the push of ego and the pull of a "more, bigger, faster" life?

Is there such a place to which she – we? – can turn inwardly and regularly: a place of calmness, assurance, hidden strength, refreshment; a place of flow that will sustain us no matter what, and which, even in times of drought in our life, will not run dry?

A Source?

It's easy to visit Mottisfont without realizing that the well-spring is there. In fact, most people come for the main attraction – the rose garden – and so they head straight past the well without even noticing it. Others walk up beside the stream without knowing that this water has just emerged, blinking and sparkling, into the light from way below ground.

The pool is humble and unspectacular. Yet without it, there would have been no monastery, no grand house, no famous rose garden… It is *the* Source for this place.

I wonder where the Source is located in the grounds of our life? Where do we go to find that simple place of reconnection between something in us and something beyond us, the place where the stirring of our soul within is answered most palpably by the calling of the Spirit of life?

* * *

If we find the Source, and if energy, inspiration – *life* – flow up and through us, then this living water will help to sustain those around us, too. We can become like a well-spring in the life of the people we know if we manage to return, time and again, to our own Source of refreshment and wisdom.

But we cannot think of this Source as ours alone, or ours to keep. Instead, we are a channel through which it may pass. "Wisdom flows from artesian springs", as the writer of Proverbs says, but we must not bottle it, or trap it, or dam it. Instead, we should simply let it pour through us and out to those who need it most.

Let it flow.

Less is More Manifesto:

I will search for the Source of my
spiritual energy, and when I find it, I
will find a way of returning to it and
drawing from it every day.

3.

Reconnecting with What is Good

We've become disconnected from each other, from the planet, from God, from ourselves. And it's not good for the soul. But how to reconnect? You can't buy the solution, or even work harder for it. Instead, our reconnection will come in many different, humble, creative forms — even, perhaps, through an act as simple as taking off our shoes. (This is holy ground, after all.)

And all is seared with trade; bleared, smeared with toil;
And wears man's smudge and shares man's smell:
    the soil
Is bare now, nor can foot feel, being shod.
(Gerard Manley Hopkins, "God's Grandeur")

What do you think of, when you hear the word
"barefoot"? Hippies? A sunny childhood? Paddling by
the sea? I suspect that most of us can only summon
memories of walking barefoot as a child, or at the
beach, because we simply don't do it at any other time.

Gerard Manley Hopkins wrote a poem called "God's
Grandeur" in 1877, about humanity, nature, and their
Creator; and in it comes this intriguing line about feet.
The "soil is bare now" (since the industrial revolution)
and *"nor can foot feel, being shod"*. This is a metaphor
for the way we have become disconnected, physically
and spiritually, from the earth – from the very ground
beneath our feet.

Since the industrial revolution we have tended to
see the earth as little more than a repository of mineral
wealth, something to fight over, grab, hold on to,
and exploit for financial gain. Such a way of seeing
diminishes us and leaves the earth bare.

So, we can wonder what we have lost. But we
can also ask appreciatively what's to be gained by
reconnecting with creation, even in small ways.
Not that we should pine nostalgically or naïvely for
a pastoral ideal that never was. Life in the natural
world is hard, and can be cruel. But we can, at least
metaphorically, take our shoes off and feel the ground
once more – and feel, as we go, for a world of seasons

and rhythms, nature and natural life; one that connects us more soulfully with who we are.

And such reconnection need not cost the earth.

* * *

Take the natural art of running (or the multi-million-pound global running industry, depending on how you look at it).

In his inspiring account of the joys and benefits of running barefoot – *Born to Run* – the runner and writer Christopher McDougall asks, in particular, why runners have slavishly worn heavily cushioned trainers – the kind that are considered normal today – since Nike "invented" them in 1972.

Such unnaturally cushioned shoes were created specifically to help runners increase their stride by allowing them to land on their heel. But this is not a natural process, and when we land on our heels we tend to damage the rest of our bodies.

Wearing heavily cushioned trainers *anyhow* causes the muscles in our feet and ankles to waste, because the shoes do the work that the feet normally do. And all the while, the shoe prevents an amazingly intricate and vital network of nerve-endings in our feet from giving crucial feedback to the brain, a process which continuously determines and fine-tunes our balance, our gait, our movement, our posture, our poise.

The architecture of the foot, writes McDougall, is "a marvel that engineers have been trying to match for centuries... Buttressing the foot's arch from all sides is a high-tensile web of twenty-six bones, thirty-three joints, twelve rubbery tendons, and eighteen muscles, all stretching and flexing like an earthquake-resistant suspension bridge."

Smother it, and it simply does not work in the way it was intended. Our feet quite literally cannot feel now, as Manley Hopkins put it, "being shod".

The Footprint

We don't *need* to "go barefoot" in order to reconnect more soulfully, of course. But it can be a powerful experience – even just taking off your shoes and having a little walk on dewy grass. Such a simple, almost foolish, ritual can reconnect you at a visceral level – beyond thinking – and help to symbolize a way of living more gently and sensitively with, and within, nature.

It might help you to reflect on your carbon footprint, too, which is both a moral and a spiritual issue in itself. And then, there is our wider footprint, too. The marks we leave on the world around us emotionally, mentally, spiritually, as we trample around.

If you walk with bare feet across wet sand you can see your own unique footprints for a short while. And then, before your very eyes, they begin to disappear, leaving no trace, in the end, of where you have been.

The tide will always come back in.

The sand will always shift in the end.

And that's how it should be, isn't it? We were not created to stamp on the earth and take what's not ours, but instead to live with it, deepening the relationship we have to each other, to the Spirit, to ourselves, and to creation.

* * *

The journey of the soul is not all about us, and never was.

"Forget not," writes Kahil Gilbran, "that the Earth delights to feel your bare feet, and the wind longs to play with your hair."

What a thought, that we can bless the *earth* itself with our presence, with something as simple as our feet, which pick their way across its surface, lightly; what a thought, that when we rediscover more of who, and how, *we* were made to be, then it has such positive effects beyond ourselves.

Life is busy, but perhaps all it takes to restart this journey of connection is one simple, slow walk across a lawn, or on wet sand, just *to feel what it's like.*

It doesn't take much.

* * *

Even Nike have woken up to the possibilities of reconnection; when Jeff Pisciotta, their senior researcher, filmed people running barefoot he was startled:

> *Instead of each foot clomping down as it would in a shoe, it behaved like an animal with a mind of its own – stretching, grasping, seeking the ground with splayed toes, gliding in for a landing like a lake-bound swan.*

Less is More Manifesto:

I will take my shoes off, every now
and again, to feel the earth beneath my
feet. I will do this as a simple act of
reconnection. And I will let it remind
me to tread lightly; to assess my carbon
footprint, to consider the mark I leave as
I go, and to walk more gently along the
path that leads home.

POETIC, POISED, AND PURPOSEFUL

1.

Distilling Your Essence

In pursuit of the "more, bigger, faster" life we can end up being defined by all the things we possess or achieve. But such "definition" is ultimately narrow and unimaginative. As we try to live more soulfully, however – in active pursuit of less – we can discover a distilled essence of ourselves which is "more" than we had previously imagined. And a very different life story begins to emerge, if we let it.

The Six Word Memoir

Your life story, in six words? Surely it's impossible.

A few years back, a magazine called *SMITH*, from the US, gave the world a compelling new form of literature. It was called the six-word memoir. The idea sprang from a tale about Ernest Hemingway, who was once challenged to write a story using only six words. Legend has it, according to the magazine, that he responded thus:

"For sale: baby shoes; never worn."

How rich even the shortest of stories can be. *Especially* the shortest. How packed full of possibility. How expressive. How demanding of your own imagination and response. How poetic.

When *SMITH* invited its readers to respond themselves by writing their own six-word memoirs, they did so, soulfully and artistically, poignantly and inspirationally.

"Cursed with cancer; blessed with friends," wrote one.

"Kind of fun, doing the impossible," went another.

"I still make coffee for two," confessed a widow.

The six-word memoir comes as a breath of fresh air, and a challenge. How many of the words about us that we deem important could be distilled yet further, like a single-malt whiskey, into an essence: short and potent?

What would your six-word memoir say about you that a full-blown biography never could?

Crafting six words is like writing an epitaph, but it need not feel as final. See it as an artistic work in progress, a snapshot in time, to be assembled with others as they develop.

(You could write one at the end of each month: put it in the diary as a recurring event, and when you pause to write and reflect, see it within the context of the others that have gone before. Like a minimalist diary.)

Such a creative process can help us to discover, express, and refine what matters to us most.

It's a chance to mine our inner story, to dig down and to listen to what's emerging from within us, instead of just relying on the props of our outward lifestyle to tell ourselves (and others) the story so far.

For there *is* another story of who we are and why we are here, if we are willing to pursue it and to express it (when we find it) dynamically through our actions.

Spiritual reflection will often unblock a sense of creativity or intuition that has lain dormant for a long time, like a seed that germinates and pushes towards the light from the darkness of the soil.

* * *

Everyone has a story…

We just don't always know what it is, until we pause to reflect on it.

Sometimes, it will take the loving care of a friend who stops to listen and who is willing to say, "Tell me your story," for it finally to germinate.

Perhaps you can be that friend for someone else.

The Defining Moment

What defines you?

It's usually the headlines from our CV that provide the defining moments of our lives. Just go to a party and try not to be asked "And what do you do?"

But when we stop to ask what matters, the good news is that we don't *have* to be defined by the headline moments alone (or at all). We are not necessarily the sum total of our qualifications, or the roles we've had, or the heights we've scaled.

Instead, it may be the smallest of details, the humblest of actions, the most disposable of throwaway lines – even things we've forgotten we've done – that help truly to define who we are.

Your life may have been shaped most profoundly by something intangible. The connection you made, for example, with ideas while reading a book. The feeling of peace you gained when you prayed. Perhaps you wrote a song that struck a chord with someone. Or you chanced upon a landscape that you would always, from then on, return to. It became a part of you. You may have met someone by chance who inspired you.

Your story could seem very different, depending on who is reading it. You are not a failure just because you didn't get the qualifications your parents hoped you would. You are not a success just because you rose highest in the ranks.

Who are you, exactly, and what could define you most truly?

* * *

At funerals we rarely cheer and praise friends or loved ones for the headings in their CV. We tend to reflect, instead, on very different things that, in looking back, have helped "define" them in our eyes: their generosity, not their riches; their humility, not their supreme intellect; their willingness to make time for us despite their busyness.

We might remember peculiar, seemingly insignificant, things that seem to sum them up beautifully: the way they danced at a party, or cheered like crazy at the football. It might be moments of kindness: the letter they bothered to write when we were low, or the time they went out of their way to help, or a wise word spoken at the right time, or when they were there when we needed a shoulder to cry on…

How might someone else remember the defining moments of *your* life? You might like to ask a friend to help you, or you might try to see your life through other people's eyes. Or through the eyes of the Spirit of life, which almost certainly sees us differently from the way we see ourselves and cares less for the outward show and more for the *heart* of a person like you or me.

For what makes us tick.

Less is More Manifesto:

I will write a six-word memoir and learn from what it says about me. Meanwhile, I will ask others to tell me their stories. I will reconsider how I define myself and others, and I will look out for how I let myself become defined.

2.

One Thing at a Time

As we find out more about who we really are, we are able to act with greater precision and authenticity in response. We may not be able to change the whole world, but we can certainly help to change the world around us. To be realistic about making a difference, however, we must focus on doing one small, simple thing at a time.

The One Thing

I'm one of those people who feels paralysed by the thought of how much needs to change in today's society in order to make the world a better place. And so often, I can end up doing nothing.

(After all, where do you start?)

Yet we live in fragile times, and doing *something* about it is better than doing nothing. In fact, it's a lot better. And in this sense, less really is more. For a start, if we all did one thing, it would amount to an awful lot more than if we all did nothing.

But also, the *little* that we focus on may prove to be the greatest discovery of our gift. None of us can do everything, anyway; but aren't we all called to do what we *can*? To do what we were put on earth to do? To act, in the way only we can act?

We must start somewhere.

So we should start with us.

You might start by changing one thing about your own life. The benefit will be felt in your home and your small action will then affect the world immediately around you as well as yourself. Perhaps, then, you can extend your reach to your road. And then to your town or city.

But unless we learn to do one, small thing after another, in the place where we are, we will do nothing at all to change the world around us.

* * *

Did you see the film *City Slickers*? Mitch (played by Billy Crystal) is a city suit from New York who has gone out West with two office friends on a cattle-driving vacation in order to find his smile. (He's just turned thirty-nine and is asking big questions about his life.) In a memorable scene he is riding out with Curly, a wise, leathery old cowboy played by Jack Palance.

Curly asks Mitch if he knows what the secret of life is, with a knowing look. Mitch replies that he doesn't. So Curly holds up one finger. The secret of life is a finger?, asks Mitch. No, says Curly: it's about discovering the "one thing" in your life.

I wonder, what is the "one thing" in your own life? We cannot do everything, after all. And when we realise that we can't, we are liberated to do *one* thing wherever we are, and to make the kind of difference to the world around us that only we can make.

If you focus on less, you may find yourself making more of your life.

The Kingfisher

As kingfishers catch fire, dragonflies draw flame…
… myself it speaks and spells,
Crying, 'What I do is me: for that I came.'
(Gerard Manley Hopkins, "As Kingfishers Catch Fire")

It's one of my favourite sights in the world, the arrow of neon iridescent blue as a kingfisher darts along a river. It's gone in a flash, but the image is burnt on the retina. For me, it represents the Spirit of life.

But Gerard Manley Hopkins, in his great poem, suggests that just as kingfishers and dragonflies do what they were created to do, so too we all manifest something divine when we can say, with conviction, "What I do is me." (Remember William the monk?)

This is not an egotistical statement: it's not saying "What I do is *for* me." In fact, it's the opposite. It's not about the ego and its desire to make something more of us than it needs to, in the form of a bigger, better identity. Instead, it is the assured stirring of the soul, which acknowledges: "for this I came."

* * *

We might say that this is our "calling". The Spirit calls and our souls answer, after all.

The poet Mary Oliver understands her own calling very simply, in terms of a metaphor. If you struggle to know what your own "one thing" is, then you may prefer, like her, to think in terms of images, instead of functions or roles. In an introduction to one of her books, she writes:

> *Poetry is a life-cherishing force. And it requires a vision, a faith, to use an old-fashioned term. For poems are not words, after all, but fires for the cold, ropes let down to the lost, something as necessary as bread in the pockets of the hungry. Yes, indeed.*

That's not hyperbole; in fact, it's a simple, clear statement. And surely it's not *just* poets who can express so vividly the gift that they bring to the world around them.

There is, I am sure, within every one of us, a way of expressing our story that will help to release our

imagination and to realize more fully our own
potential, a way that is not just "words, after all",
but fire, and rope, and bread.

The Flower on the Pavement
Here is one more metaphor that might help.

The psychologist and wilderness guide Bill
Plotkin uses a powerful but fragile analogy to
describe the way our soulfulness will still rise up,
almost despite ourselves.

"Even in our synthetic, egocentric society,"
he writes, "the soul stirs in our subterranean
depths, endlessly calling, pushing up like a flower
through the cracks in the concrete pavement of
our lives."

Our true selves can be paved over by hurt,
by wounds, by busyness, by defensiveness, by
materialism, by disconnection, by frenzy, by
selfishness, by the accumulation of more stuff...

And yet, despite all the concrete, still the soul
stirs and pushes up through the cracks like a
flower reaching towards the light. Consider what
the flower might represent for you:

Something that makes you come alive, perhaps?

Something people come to you for, time and
again?

Something you do effortlessly, without even
realizing you're doing it?

Something that sets you apart, a unique facet to
your identity?

You may have been doing your "one thing" for years without even realizing it. You may have rushed past the flower on the pavement and not noticed it; but still, it is there, growing up through.

It's odd to think that we may not yet have been fully introduced to the person we were created to be. But this very moment of clarity – in itself – should encourage us to keep going, along the narrow path that takes us further into the heart of life itself.

Less is More Manifesto:

I will stop trying to change the world, and instead I will try to change the world around me, by finding one thing I would love to do, and doing it — locally. It may not be spectacular, but it will touch at least one other soul. As I go, I will reflect on how, like the kingfisher, I can be me, doing the thing for which I came. And I will look out for flowers on the concrete pavement of my life.

3.

The Way We Live

The content of our lives may surprise us when we stop to reflect upon it, as we have already considered. But it's not enough simply to reflect – the emerging inner story of our lives then requires an outer form in order for us to express it within the world. The outer form is not about our superficial appearance, however: it is about the way we act.

Life as Art?

The writer Ben Okri suggests:

> *Nothing can live in art or in life that does not find*
> *the form unique to itself by which its individual soul*
> *can be expressed... For the outer condition of life must*
> *correspond to the inner, and the outer condition of form*
> *must correspond to the inner condition of the work, its*
> *content, its dream...*

The word, if you like, must be made flesh. The inside of our life needs a form in which to express itself to the outside.

There is an artistry to life, then, that we often neglect in our fast-paced rush for what is "more, bigger, faster". We dash, like it's every man and woman for themselves. But there is another way to live, a poetic way, if you like, which – with an economy of expression – inspires others on their way.

* * *

"True poets," writes Okri, "just want you to honour the original pact you made with the universe when you drew your first breath from the unseen magic in the air."

That's all.

The Gesture

So how do we live "poetically"? You may feel as if you have a hundred and one things to get done, today. But here is a suggestion. Try to live for just this one day of your life gesture by gesture, instead of task by task.

Call it an experiment. Who knows where it might lead you?

To make this simpler, try to think about something outside your usual routine. Take, for example, the kind of rhythm you might find on a really good holiday. You might, once you had taken a few days to slow yourself down, get into the simple routine of (for instance) buying the paper, having a coffee and a croissant, taking a swim, having lunch, enjoying a nap, going for a walk, heading out for dinner, having a drink, returning for an evening stroll by the water...

It's not so hard to think how you can live "gesture by gesture" through such a day, moving more slowly, deliberately, positively, without rushing or getting stressed.

If only we could make that kind of progress – with its more soulful rhythms and routines – through the everyday maelstrom. Gesture by gesture.

Perhaps we can.

* * *

Living like this would certainly gives us a different route from morning to night.

We tend to divide our days into tasks to be completed (or problems to be solved). What are you up to, for the rest of the day? Write yourself a quick plan, on paper or in your head. And just notice, for a moment, how you see your day developing.

You may be on your lunch break and thinking about getting back to work, for example. Normally your mind would be turning to the next task in hand and your inner momentum would be pulling you back towards it, probably quite hard.

But perhaps you have a sandwich to finish, first. A sandwich you may not often stop to chew properly. Stop to savour it, for once, as a simple gesture of good taste.

There may be a person who has served you that sandwich, whom you could talk to, and say goodbye to before you move on as a gesture of thanks.

There may be a short walk back to your office, which normally you would walk quickly, and perhaps tensely, as your mind went into overdrive, the adrenaline kicked in, and your stress levels rose. Instead, you might walk a little more slowly, as a gesture of calmness and presence.

You may even stop to notice the colours, smells, or sounds that have become so familiar you hardly ever stop to realize you are *here*. Today, instead, you could stop a moment longer to notice – as a gesture to yourself – that you *are* here, in this time and place.

It's a different way to get from A to B. And the danger is, it might not even get you to B at all. But that is a risk you may have to take.

The Pose

Moving gesture by gesture is not about maintaining an act; it's about developing posture.

So how is your posture? Is it defensive? Threatening? Hurried? Do you have a closed posture? (Sometimes I catch myself adopting the crash position.) An open one? Are you steady, or off balance?

Posture often comes with a pose. And we strike a pose to help us survive. It may be the pose demanded by our role – as a successful business person, or a busy parent, or an ambitious student...

But once the façade has been created, we must then spend time and energy working to maintain it, to prevent our mask from slipping. We find we have to keep the pose going, to keep ourselves going. And all the while, the pose will leave us feeling tense, stressed, tightly coiled...

Not ourselves.

* * *

Imagine, instead of striking a pose, that you exhibit *poise*. The poise, perhaps, of a ballet dancer, or a skilful sportsperson, or an inspirational leader.

Poise speaks of balance, composure, *readiness*.

Yet those who demonstrate poise tend to be rare, sadly. It's a reflection on the world we have created, that demands we "look busy" (even if we're not) instead of living with grace.

If you could spend one day in perfect poise, how different would it feel? And imagine if those around you were inspired by your example to do likewise. When we find our poise, there is less need, after all, for anyone around us to strike a pose back. Poise can be positively contagious.

* * *

Dancing reminds us that life doesn't have to be one mad rush to the finishing line.

No one dances in order to get from one place to another. You don't dance to get somewhere more quickly or expediently, either. No one takes to the dance floor at point A with a view to finishing their dance at point B. It's not *about* where you get to so much as the grace with which you get there.

It's the beauty of the movement, the fluidity, the chemistry, the rhythm, the collaboration, the inspiration. Another way of moving.

A beautiful dance usually requires poise. So if you were to "dance" metaphorically through today, how would you like to move? How would it affect your sense of flow, and how differently might you carry yourself through your work and your play?

A dance requires more than one person, too. It requires that we find our rhythm with others, and move in step with them. Co-operating, not competing, to help each other find our poise.

The ultimate dance is between our soul, on the inside, and the Spirit of life, beyond us; and if we let these two keep in step *through* us then we will find the unforced rhythms that we quietly crave.

Inner Poise

Pose is about the veneer, the surface; poise, on the other hand, comes from the inside out. And it's *inner* poise that touches the outside world most profoundly.

Below the surface, then, the soul stirs us; a still, small voice speaks; and the person we were truly created to be waits, *poised*: balanced, assured, and at peace. We glimpse that person so rarely; yet it's he or she who we must ask to lead us in the dance – and not the panicky voice of our insecure, ego-driven mind which tells us to keep up appearances.

"Your True Self," writes Richard Rohr, "is… 'the face you had before you were born', as the Zen masters say." Our life's quest is not to perfect the pose, but to become the face of that true self, and to discover the presence and poise that come with it. When we find these, we will cease to strive, because striving necessarily comes from trying to prove that we are someone we are not.

Less is More Manifesto:

I will try living poetically — gesture by gesture — and see where it takes me. I will pose less, and return instead to a state of inner poise which will help to shape the way I live — its form — from the inside out.

4.

Learning to See Each Other Differently

If we cease relating to each other as poser relates to poser – constantly judging others from the surface – then we will have less need for the layers we use to hide behind. And when we stop trying to use our relationships principally to get what we can from others, we are free to give the very best of ourselves to the world around us, fearlessly and with love.

The Statue in the Stone

Most of us judge each other relentlessly (not always badly, but we make constant judgments, nevertheless). We form opinions rapidly, often based on presuppositions, or prejudices; we see things we like or dislike about other people or the ideas they espouse, and we make our call. We put them in a box. We mark their cards.

But what, exactly, are we judging? Think about it from your own perspective: you present yourself to the world as best you can, through what you wear, how you come across, the way you speak, all of that.

And then others, who see the world through their own lens, judge you. They form an opinion, frequently based not on the truth of who you are, but on the idea they have just formed about you. On their perception.

It might be based on hearsay, or first impressions, or just the way you're coming across at any given moment. But I will judge my impression of you, and you will judge your impression of me, and really we will not be judging each other at all, but the perception of who we think the other is instead.

Is that the way to understand, to relate to one another, to live peacefully, and to love?

* * *

"Judge not, lest ye be judged," said Jesus, for good reason. When we stop judging, we free others to be themselves, and we in turn become free from the fear of who they might be.

And if we learn to accept ourselves, and each other, more truly for who we are, without illusion and through the eyes of love, we may also learn how to see through the layers of superficiality we present to each other.

As we do so, we give ourselves a better chance of accepting *each other* for who we are. It works both ways. It becomes, not a vicious circle of judgment, but a virtuous circle of love.

* * *

There is an art to seeing people for who they truly are. Michelangelo knew it when he said:

In every block of marble, I see a statue as plain as though it stood before me, shaped and perfect in attitude and action. I have only to hew away the rough walls that imprison the lovely apparition to reveal it to the other eyes as mine see it.

There is Nothing You Have That I Need

It's hard to relate to others when something such as status, or religion, or money, or history, or social background creates a barrier between us.

Why is it that we act differently (whether negatively or positively) the moment we discover that the person we're talking to is famous, or the CEO of a big company, for example – as if *what they have* makes them more significant, or more powerful, or to be feared, or more worthy of our attention?

In the spiritual sense, we are all rich beyond compare, if we did but realise it. We are complete in the way we have been created to be, and there is no material thing that can alter for good or ill who we truly are. So there is nothing I have that you need, and there is nothing you have that I need.

We can therefore relate to each other without agenda, and may share freely what we have, and who we are, without fear of loss or the covert desire to gain.

In other words, we can be free to be our self, and to allow others to do likewise. Once we understand this very simple piece of wisdom, it should mean that we relate more readily, truthfully, and lovingly to each other.

The less I want from you, the more I'll find I have to offer, and the more we will both receive from the exchange.

Less is More Manifesto:

I will stop being so judgmental of others, especially of their outward appearance. Each time I meet someone new, I will try to remember that he or she has nothing I need and act accordingly. I will try to see the beauty of the statue within the rough-hewn blocks around me, and I will allow the Sculptor of life to chip away at my own rough edges.

FOCUSED, FIGHTING, AND FREE

1.

Walking the Narrow Path

At this point on our journey – as we ask what
it means to live a life of less and seek to discover
more in the process – let's remember that we have
determined to set out on a different path. We have
left home – the world as we know it – in order
to find our home (our true place in the world).
Instead of using our minds alone, like a twitching
compass, to try to guide us, we seek instead to live
more soulfully, and choose within each moment to
find our true North, as a gyroscope guides a ship, free
from outside interference. That is the path we seek.

The Labyrinth

Once, I guided a group of bemused teenagers around the ancient labyrinth that lies at the top of a hill close to where I live. (I'd been invited to do so by their teacher, who was looking for a way of introducing them to another way of seeing their spiritual path.)

Walking a labyrinth can be a profound and symbolic exercise if you do it reflectively. You can't get lost in a labyrinth such as the one I often walk; it's not a maze, even though it looks a bit like one; instead, there's a single path "in", which leads you all the way to the very centre – and there's a single path back out again.

People have, for centuries, used labyrinths to symbolize their pilgrimage of life – towards God, who lies at the very centre of all things. But I also use the labyrinth simply to invite people to reflect on what lies at their centre, too. And it was an interesting process for the young people.

They were sceptical about it at first, as you might expect; but after we'd made the walk and found our way to the centre of the labyrinth, we had a profound chat about what it is we might find buried within us. Our passions. Our values. Our beliefs.

Treasure?

And the thing that struck these youngsters more than anything, was that they had never been invited or challenged to think like that before. Instead, their young minds had already been primed to think about how they could "get

somewhere" in life – inner momentum was building –
and how successful they could outwardly become.

The trajectory of the labyrinth is entirely different:
an utterly "other" way of seeing the path in front of
us, which physically slows its walker down into the
present moment, and requires that we travel step by
step towards a richer destination. A different way of
imagining how life could turn out.

* * *

A funny thing happens, in my experience, when we
move closer to the centre. The excess baggage we carry
with us – the masks, the outfits, the war-paint, the
poses – it all begins to seem so insignificant.

We must come as we are to the centre.

And therein lies a deep and beautiful mystery, which
demands, ultimately, that we relinquish "the things
that we have carried here", as the songwriter Martyn
Joseph puts it so touchingly.

The things that we have carried here –
One day they will disappear…
Beautiful… We can be beautiful.
And we can be free.

This is no senseless journey. The path invites us to let
go of what weighs us down. The narrow path leads
home, to the centre of life.

Less is More Manifesto:

I will check with myself and recheck
— which path am I walking? Which way
am I travelling? Is it towards "more,
bigger, faster" — directed by the often
skewed compass of my mind — or towards
the centre of life, guided by the nudge
of soul and the call of the Spirit?

2.

To Freedom

Nothing and no one is stopping us from living more lightly, more joyfully, more freely – apart from us, and the choices we make for ourselves. For those of us who live in the "free" world, we have an added responsibility to exercise the freedom we enjoy. For those who live in all kinds of captivity, there is still freedom – perhaps the most noble freedom of all – to choose to act in grace and love, whatever the circumstances.

The Volunteer

"Freedom needs a volunteer," Martyn Joseph goes on to sing in that same, wonderful song "The Things That We Have Carried Here". It's a powerful, challenging line. For who is willing to stand up and volunteer for the kind of freedom that means walking a narrow path, travelling lightly, coming *as we are*, carrying less? Who dares to give it a go?

Freedom *is* within our grasp. Yet it requires that we find the courage to break out of the kind of life we are expected to live, of unquestioning consumerism, of ecological ignorance, of selfish gain.

Part of the problem, perhaps, is that we have simply forgotten what true freedom means, beyond being able to do what we like, when we like. But there is more to freedom than that.

* * *

In Maya Angelou's famous poem "Caged Bird", she describes two types of bird: the bird that is free, and the bird that is caged.

The free bird has a choice. It could stand outside its cage, but never truly taste the freedom it already has. Potentially, it could stay put and never use its wings, let alone take off and discover the hidden lands that lie over the horizon.

In the poem, however, the bird does take flight, and it uses all the space and the freedom it has at its disposal. I wonder if we would dare to do the same. Surely, something rises in us at such a thought, just as it does, perhaps, if we look up to see a bird flying free in the summer sky, and we dream of swapping our own cares for its carefree soaring. It's funny how, in a go-getting world, we may like to think that "the sky's the limit", when really our fear of flying keeps us earthbound.

Freedom needs a volunteer. And if we stand outside the cage – if nothing is stopping us but our own fear, or avarice, or lack of imagination – then we have a responsibility to *be* free. To live differently, if that's what we feel stirred to do and, at the very least, to try small acts of creative subversion which may help us to stretch our own wings and encourage others to do the same.

What takes courage, for you? Going home from work on time? Then do it. Speaking to a neighbour, and inviting him or her round? Then do it. Switching off the computer? Then do it. Walking barefoot? Then do it. Spending time doing nothing, for a change, watching clouds? Then do it!

* * *

The caged bird, on the other hand, has no choice. Often people find themselves in grave situations: they have poor health, or are born into poverty, or literal captivity, or political tyranny.

Nevertheless, her caged bird, in glorious defiance, still chooses to sing. If it can do nothing else, it can do that. Defiantly, perhaps. And this caged bird shows us still further possibilities of freedom.

Even in the most dire of situations, such as the philosopher Victor Frankl experienced in the Second World War death camp of Auschwitz, we can choose to exercise the most potent kind of freedom available to us.

"When we are no longer able to change a situation," Frankl writes, "… we are challenged to change ourselves." We can learn from any situation, whether we have control over it or not, and we have the freedom to change *through* it for the better. The human being is "a deciding being", as he calls it. And so we *always* have the freedom to act in grace, and to respond in love, wherever we find ourselves.

He recalls watching men giving away their last pieces of bread to others. And he saw enough examples – often heroic – to suggest that people always have what he describes as the *spiritual* freedom to choose how to act. Even in a concentration camp, the human being, he considers, has the choice to act with dignity through an inner decision.

And these small, yet monumentally significant, choices determine our path.

"Between stimulus and response there is a space," he concludes. "In that space is our power to choose our response. In our response lies our growth and our freedom."

This is a freedom that reaches to the sky even in the most confined and oppressive of spaces. In fact, Frankl seems to suggest that it's *especially* when we have less apparent freedom to exercise that we discover so much more.

* * *

Freedom to Fail

One thing to remember about freedom, however, is that fear stops us from living. So let's remember we have one particular freedom that seems almost forgotten within today's culture in particular: the freedom to *fail*.

In fact, we grow through failure. That's one of the counter-intuitive lessons we struggle to learn from a culture geared towards "success". We must free ourselves to fail gloriously, by experimenting with new ways of being, by being creative in our thinking and courageous in our actions, dreaming new dreams of a better path to walk through life!

How many times have you failed, recently, in the pursuit of living with greater freedom, lightness, joy, energy, communion, passion, creativity, and wonder? If I have not failed in my pursuit of such beautiful things then, chances are, I have not tried to pursue them.

If it's hard to imagine being free to fail, perhaps you can start by allowing a colleague, family member, or friend to fail first; by offering them the hand of grace you may yet grow to fail yourself.

Less is More Manifesto:

I will volunteer for freedom by breaking out of the norm, trying small acts of creative subversion, and remembering that I am free to choose how I respond to every situation I face. And I will dare to fail more frequently in pursuit of a life well lived.

3.

Keep Fighting

The idea of living with greater freedom is all very well, but the reality of life-as-we-know-it has a way of crushing the dream. Get real, it says. You're too busy. You can't do things differently. Life isn't like that. Go back to your work and be quiet. So now we know: we have a fight on our hands. This is the time to remember we have a role to play in the fight for life.

The Battle

The story goes that when Winston Churchill's finance minister approached him, during the Second World War, to argue for a cut in funding to the arts, Churchill replied, very simply, "Then what are we fighting *for*?"

It's a question we ought to ask of ourselves, often. Because we're all involved in a battle for something. We just forget what it was we were fighting for in the first place.

* * *

In 2011, a "summit against violent extremism" was called, at which a group of former neo-Nazis, Islamic fundamentalists, and drugs gang members gathered to discuss what makes young people turn to violence. It was run by Google Ideas.

Susan Cruz, once a member of a notorious LA gang herself, spoke, ahead of the event, about the similarities between people of different cultures who end up living lives of violence. She said:

> *They may dress different, their language may be different but fundamentally deep down inside the child that joins a drugs gang in the US is the same child that joins a militia or an extremist religious group, and becomes a suicide bomber.*

"They are all," she says, "looking for the same things."

If she's right, the question is, what *are* they looking for?

No doubt there are many different angles to explore, ranging from the psychological, to the sociological, to the anthropological, all with helpful views on why people need things like meaning, identity and purpose in their lives.

Yet, from a spiritual perspective, we could also suggest that they are looking, quite simply, for a fight.

And while few of us turn to violent extremism, we are *all* somewhere on the spectrum of aggression, not necessarily because we are bad people, but because an energy flows through us that is warrior-like, whether we like it or not.

* * *

The spiritual writer John Eldredge suggests that our human impulse to fight is not a bad thing, despite where it so often seems to lead us.

In fact, he argues, most of the great stories that stir and captivate our hearts involve a battle between light and dark, good and evil.

"Why does every story have a villain?" he writes. "It's hard to think of a tale without one. As children, we learned to fear the Big Bad Wolf, and the Troll under the bridge. And as we grew older, we discovered more serious villains..."

Every story has a villain, he suggests, "because yours does".

The great stories stir us because we know, deep down, that we are involved in a battle for *something*. A little girl watches a film such as *Star Wars* and something within her believes that she, too, can fight, like Princess Leah, against all that is wrong with the world. The impulse within her is that she, too, has a part to play.

It is the gentle, yet assuredly powerful, impulse of soul which inspires her, and which runs counter to the ego's insecure and aggressive demand for self-reliance and security. The soul does not want you to duck conflict; it just wants you to choose the right battles to fight.

Somewhere along the line, in the push for "more, bigger, faster", we forgot what it was we were fighting for. Perhaps Mother Teresa, that most pugnacious of battlers, can help direct our fire.

"Life is life," she wrote. "Fight for it."

Soldier or Warrior?

So, this is serious: we are fighting for our lives. And "aggression is in all of us," agrees the spiritual writer Matthew Fox in his book *The Hidden Spirituality of Men*. "Whether athlete or preacher, businessperson or taxi driver, aggression will emerge at some point."

It's easy, he suggests, to identify the negative ways that aggression expresses itself: as war, as conquest (in business or in sex), as passivity (aggression turned against oneself: "I can't do that…"), as selfish competition ("I can't win unless you lose"), and much more.

But what are the soulful ways to engage our aggressive impulse? This is where the difference between – as we understand them – a soldier and a warrior comes in.

Soldiers have to follow orders. Kill or be killed. No choice. You are part of an army, and must obey the orders you receive.

Warriors, however, must follow their hearts, and the path they walk is towards life, through love.

Love is the overriding ethic of warriors, who will fight in almost every sense but the physical, literal one – unless they have to. They will fight through the example of their lives; they will fight with control, patience, grace, and understanding, in order to demonstrate the way of love itself, which is a narrow path to walk. It takes guts to go against the flow, after all.

Think of the example of people such as Mother Teresa, who fought for justice for the poor by living among the poorest; think of Gandhi, who fought the might of empire with that most threatening of weapons, non-violence. Think of Martin Luther King, who nurtured a dream and fought with vision. Warriors.

* * *

Perhaps the most inspiring way we can fight is with *creativity* – which Matthew Fox suggests is "the weapon, the sword, of the true spiritual warrior".

Creativity helps to define a spiritual warrior, who, in Fox's poetic words, "digs deep into a wellspring of wildness that provides the energy for new life, new connections, new images, and new moral imagination by which to change things in a deep, not superficial way."

Now *that's* a reason to enter the battle.

The true warrior, he suggests, is "a co-creator, a worker with Spirit, a worker for Spirit. The warrior's hands are the hands of Spirit at work; the warrior's mind is seized by Spirit precisely in the work of creativity."

They work with the Spirit which hovered over the face of the waters, in the beginning, and breathed life into being.

"Every warrior is an artist," concludes Fox, "an artist at work for the people that they might live."

Less is More Manifesto:

I will choose which battles to fight, and channel my deep impulse to enter the fray on the side of what is right; on the side of the Spirit of life. And I will fight like a warrior, with creativity, in the name of love.

AWARE, AWAKE, AND ALIVE

1.

Tuning Back in

As we pursue the road home, it takes application
to stay the course; discipline. We must continue
to listen for the call of the Spirit of life, to seek
its guiding, and to live in a heightened state of
awareness. If we do, the reward is great. We will
discover that things aren't always what they seem.
That life was here for the living, all along.

The Lamp-Post

Where do we look for help, for meaning, for salvation, even, within our overdriven world? Sometimes we can kid ourselves that we are searching when actually we're not. It will take tenacious souls to really look for signs of life within this culture, and to go after them.

An old story helps to illustrate this:

There was a once a man who spent too much time at the bar one night, and was found crawling around under a street light by a passer-by.

"What's going on?" the passer-by asks.

"I lost my watch," the fellow says.

"Well," says the passer-by, "I'll help you look for it."

After ten minutes, the passer-by says, "Look, it's clear your watch is not here. Are you sure this is where you dropped it?"

"Oh no," says the watch-less man, "I dropped it down the street."

"Then why in heaven's name are you looking for it here?"

"Because the light is better."

* * *

We give ourselves the greatest opportunity to find what we're looking for when we are looking in roughly the right place. And so we owe it to ourselves to step away from the lamp-post and search as if we really mean it.

The Signal

The shy, delicate Spirit of life whispers, prompts, and stirs without fuss. It is *not* clamouring for attention, or striking a pose, or trying to compete.

Instead, perhaps, it's a kingfisher arrowing along a river, or a deer peeping from behind a tree; perhaps it's a wave that's just broken, or a morning mist that lifted even before we've awakened to glimpse how magical the world had looked beneath her veil.

* * *

Here is a gift of true worth: divine presence. Amid the white noise of a world surfing the airwaves; amid the narrow-casts, broadcasts, and podcasts; caught in the radio signals, mobile downloads, and webcasts; up with the static and the crackle of interference... one simple signal still pulses from ages past, like a heartbeat:

Are you receiving me?

Are you receiving me?

Are you receiving me?

The Pianist

The writer Paulo Coelho speaks of the time he was walking through a shopping centre with his friend Ursula, a violinist. Suddenly she gripped his arm and said, "Listen!" Over the voices of adults talking, children screaming, heels clicking and tinny Muzak, Ursula could hear the faintest sound of a piano being played.

As he attuned his ears, Coelho also began to discern the strains of Chopin, Schubert, and Mozart.

Eventually, they discovered the pianist on a little stage, tucked away. A notice said that he was a famous musician from Georgia. Having come to Britain looking for work, it seemed he had ended up here, at the fag-end of a shopping mall.

"Except, I'm not sure he really is here," Coelho writes. "His eyes are fixed on the magical world where the music was composed; [while] his hands share with us all... the very best of himself."

In other words, he is connected, in tune, and utterly tuned in; and as such, he is also able to connect those around him – those, at least, who are willing to tune in to another world, too.

Sadly, no one, aside from the two friends, stopped. Such is the nature of our world. Everyone was busy shopping, or passing through from one place to another.

Nevertheless, the pianist didn't seem to notice whether anyone was watching. Instead, he was "conversing with Mozart's angels", as Coelho puts it.

Coelho considers this a divine encounter within the dullest, most bereft of places: "God is in the soul, and in the hands of this man," he concludes.

It's a moving story. The pianist serves as a reminder to us all. He plays as if he's at Carnegie Hall because this is his joy, his reason for living. And Ursula reminds us, too, that if we are listening carefully, attuned to the divine within the ordinariness of it all, then we can notice another melody flowing beneath – or, let's say, above – all of the background music of life.

Variation on a Theme

A few years ago, in a well-documented experiment, the virtuoso violinist Joshua Bell went to L'Enfant Plaza metro station in Washington in the middle of the rush hour, took out his violin (handcrafted by Antonio Stradivari), and began to play.

He was used to playing at the world's greatest concert halls, not busking. (Three days before, he had sold out the Boston Symphony Hall.) Dressed in jeans, a long-sleeved T-shirt, and a baseball cap, he began by playing the chaconne from Bach's Partita No. 2 in D minor.

According to Wikipedia, in the next forty-five minutes 1,097 people passed by, but only seven paused for a minute or more to watch him. 1,090 others didn't stop for a second as they brushed past one of the world's greatest violinists.

This is not to condemn those busy commuters (everyone's trying to get somewhere, after all), nor to berate ourselves for rushing (or perhaps sleep-walking) through life. But think, for a moment, how much better our life could become, and how much richer, if we stop to see what is going on right in front of our very eyes.

We might rightly ask ourselves how much we are missing. But putting it more positively, how much more do we still have to discover?

* * *

Recently I received a note from a man called Stuart – a professional singer – who'd been receiving a series of daily advent e-mails I'd been writing. I'd been encouraging my participants to keep an eye out for what they might be missing, even within the most drab or dreary circumstances. Here's what he noticed that particular day:

"I had some domestic chores to do, and needed to go to the supermarket. I needed to get some cash out, it was cold, and I was stressed and a bit irked through lack of sleep (I have a seventeen-month-old little boy). As I stood in the queue at the cash machine, I became aware of a young girl who was stood in front of me with her mum. While her mum was getting her money, the girl was singing away to herself. And I found myself tuning in to what she was singing.

"As they walked away, I heard the girl singing very simply and quietly: 'This little light of mine, I'm going to let it shine. This little light of mine, I'm going to let it shine...' My spirit lifted, I broke into a smile, and have been pretty much singing that little song ever since."

* * *

Close Your Eyes

I find it very useful to spend time outdoors in reflection. This need not be for long, but it helps me to build a rhythm of deliberate "retreat" into my life. It's a way of regularly taking a little time out to tune back in.

This sort of spiritual discipline not only benefits us at the time; it increases our level of awareness throughout our day, and helps us to notice more of what's emerging around us, and within us.

Here's a very simple – yet powerful – exercise to try when you are next outdoors with a few moments to spare. This process is particularly helpful because it reconnects our inside (soul) with the outside (Spirit) in a way that doesn't involve *thinking* too hard about anything. It leaves the compass out of it, and engages the gyroscope instead.

"It suffices," writes the author Richard Benson, "to *stop and close your eyes for a full minute.*" Simple as that.

"Listen, smell, feel, suck the air in," he continues, "and the place enters you in a way that it cannot when you merely stand admiring a view…"

In closing our eyes, we become more aware of our *feeling* for what's there. And as we do so, we are able to stop rationally interpreting everything around us, or consuming it (even as a spiritual experience), and let our senses connect with it in a visceral way.

And we may, at last, be better able to welcome the shy, delicate Spirit of Life as such, as it whispers, and prompts, and stirs us gently, without fanfare.

On its terms, not our own.

Less is More Manifesto:

I will stop to listen to buskers, as a simple reminder that there is always more to this world than meets the eye. I will practise using my senses, to become more fully aware of what I'm still missing. I will get outdoors more often, and engage with the "outside world" at a visceral level. And I will learn to sense the divine presence of the Spirit, wherever I find myself.

2.

The Promise of Things to Come

Even in the smallest and seemingly most humble details of Creation – like a leaf falling from a tree, or a butterfly settling on a flower – we can sense the powerful promise of things to come. Our journey must, inevitably, lead us through times of loss, but in learning to let go, the path will bring us back to life.

The Tree in Autumn

Nature speaks to us at the deepest levels of both life and death. The two are forever linked, in a never-ending, seasonal expression of the way the universe has been set up to work. But even within the more melancholic passages of the year – especially as summer fades to autumn, when the evenings draw in and the leaves begin to fall from the trees – we have so much more to savour, and to appreciate, when we stop to notice.

Did you know, for example, that the trees in autumn use the season to purge and purify themselves of toxins? Just before the leaves fall from their branches, trees will shift their natural "waste" into them. That's partly why they turn to such dazzling colours.

If we – as people – managed to produce anything like the incredible outward display of a tree in autumn then we would almost certainly be reluctant to let go of our fabulous array. After all, it draws attention to us, validates us, even. We would probably hold on to it for dear life, saying, "Look what I did!"

And yet, the trees shed their beauty, in a perfectly natural way, in preparation for the next season. They allow themselves to be laid bare in order to prepare for renewal.

In shedding, they make space for new growth, and simultaneously find themselves purified.

Season after season, we can learn from a Creation which is not afraid to let go in order to let come. Even what seems to us like death contains the tantalising promise of things to come.

The Death before Death

Ultimately, every act of letting go, however small, points us through death, and back to life again.

Let's think one final time, then, about our relationship to our things, and consider the great spiritual mystery of how we can die in order to live, much more fully.

Remember that our ego needs to identify with many external things in order to create a sense of some kind of "self" for us. This useful list, from Eckhart Tolle's *The Power of Now*, helps to remind us of the things we use to fashion our superficial identity:

> ... *possessions, the work you do, social status and recognition, knowledge and education, physical appearance, special abilities, relationships, personal and family history, belief systems, and often also political, nationalistic, racial, religious, and other collective identifications.*

Our ego will try, at all times, to defend and feed that sense of self, *to keep it alive at all costs*, if you like – which is quite unlike the tree in autumn!

But here is the beauty of compiling such a comprehensive list.

"None of these is you," Tolle writes.

(In other words, you are not your ego.)

"Do you find this frightening? Or is it a relief to know this?" he asks. For the truth is, we will have to relinquish all of these things sooner rather than later...

"Death is a stripping away of all that is not you," he concludes. "The secret of life is to 'die before you die' – and find that there is no death."

And find that there is no death.

The Inkling

The signs of life are all around us.

"I have struggled," writes Michael McCarthy, for the *Independent*, "to find a way of expressing my elation at seeing... the first butterfly of the year." What great joy, for those who are in tune with the seasons, and Creation, and with their place within it all!

"It was a brimstone, a bright yellow brimstone," he continues. "Using science, and rationality, I can tell you quite a lot about it: that it was an insect; that it belonged to the butterfly family *Pieridae*, the whites... that in its caterpillar stage it had fed on the plants buckthorn or alder buckthorn; and that it had hibernated disguised as a leaf, probably in an ivy clump, until the first warm day in March woke it up."

But that doesn't *really* describe it, he muses. That brimstone "electrified me instantly; it was the sign of the turning year, not just of the warm times coming again but of the great rebirth of everything, the great unstoppable renewal, and the brilliance of its colour seemed to proclaim the magnitude of the change it was signalling."

Such a simple, fragile creature, yet such a profound glimpse of the Spirit of life, fluttering unremarkably, save in the eyes of those who glimpse its flickering radiance. The soul stirs and moves us, deep into the turning of a season and the delightful promise of "more".

* * *

This reminds me of a time when I was walking through the countryside with my father, in the late afternoon sunshine. We'd already savoured the spectacle of a buzzard circling low, and a heron hauling itself up and away like something prehistoric from a lake. But what thrilled us the most was the unmistakable silhouette, against the blue sky above us, of the first swallow of the year.

It was such a tiny signal of what was to come – my thoughts raced to cricket, fresh-cut grass, rivers, beer gardens, sunsets – but one that touched our souls in a way that left us walking in cheerful, contemplative silence for a few moments, buoyed by a shared inkling.

The turning of the year, the rebirth of *everything*, the great unstoppable renewal… I'd say Michael McCarthy did a pretty good job of describing what we *can* sense, deep down, on the kind of day when the world spins towards the light, a season turns before our eyes, and we feel that fathomless, visceral knowing that everything will one day be made new.

Less is More Manifesto:

I will allow the simplest, most powerful signs to draw me closer to the heart of Life, to that which I may call home. I'll let the colours of the trees remind me, each autumn, that we have to let go, in the end, to let come. And I will begin, today, the process of dying, so that I can come alive. So that I may be born again.

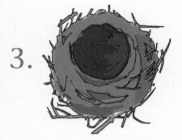

3.

Back to Life

---

*The end is a new beginning. And as we near
the conclusion of this particular journey, we
find ourselves back where we started: with a
challenge to leave "home" and all it represents,
and to act upon what we have discovered. But
what will help us to depart? Where will we
go? How will we navigate our way? Perhaps
we can draw inspiration from the birds.*

"What must it be like," asks the author Tim Dee, "to be so sensitive to the magnetism of the earth that you are able to taste the iron in the air; to be drawn up in to that air, as if evaporated; to feel the inching creep of longer nights pushing you away from what you know, towards what you don't?"

He is writing about the miracle and mystery of migrating birds. And in his acclaimed book *The Running Sky* he describes exquisitely the wonder of watching them on the wing. You must have seen such birds passing overhead, or stopping for a well-earned rest, or settling in for the season.

The real wonder, however, lies in how these tiny birds manage to *know* – without weather forecasts or calendars – when to arrive and when to leave, and where to go when they do. That's especially so when it comes to their very first flight. After all, they don't get a manual, or a sat-nav, or a crash-course in orienteering.

It's all built in, according to Dee. They already have everything they need, miraculously, for the journey home that lies ahead.

"What must it be like to hatch from an egg," asks Dee, "and look up from a nest and know the stars already, as if your paper-thin skull were a planetarium, along with the smooth curve of your late-abandoned egg shell and the cup of your nest, too, as if the skies and the stars had pressed their map into everything there is of you?"

What must it be like? How wonderful.

We may not have such a map, but we do have a precision instrument like the ship's gyroscope, which, for us, will realign us with what matters, point us towards true north, and help us to stay the course. The Spirit of life calls to us – that indeed there is more to life than "this" – and our soul responds with urgency and joy: Believe it! It's true! And so we are offered the prospect of our own great journey, our own epic flight into the unknown.

We are born, like the birds, with an instinct: to go. To leave home, when the time is right, in search of our home again. To be "drawn up into that air" and to fly.

* * *

And that is where we now find ourselves: standing at this particular end, with a new beginning before us, it is time to take wing. To taste freedom.

There must be more to life than this.

You are invited to set out, to search for a treasure that all the money in the world cannot buy. To find a way that transcends all known formulae. This is the journey no one can force you to make, yet the journey that Love, and Life itself compel you to take.

It is the path that leads us beyond ourselves, yet inexorably back towards the centre of who we are. The road which takes us from life, through death, and back to life again...

It is a finding, and a losing.

A growing, and a shedding.

A calling, and a listening.

A letting go, and a receiving.

An arrival, and a departure.

The end is just the beginning. We are born, and born again.

Born with nothing, once more, into everything.

Seeing, once more, and with fresh eyes, everything that was already here, everything that we could not see for looking when we set out to discover it.

Seeing, after all, that we are already rich.

That we have all we possibly need.

That nothing we can take for ourselves can add to the person we were born to become.

And that nothing can be taken away.

Go well.

Less is More Manifesto:

I will leave the nest. I will set out.
I will trust my instinct. I will fly.

Epilogue:
The Spanner

Despite being told off by the doorman for wearing a woolly hat in the cathedral (it *was* winter, after all), I was ready to savour the delights of the annual service of nine lessons and carols: a world-class cathedral choir; a gorgeous, candle-lit atmosphere; a snowy setting; a menu of mouth-watering anthems and spine-tingling solos; the pageantry of the choristers; a towering, twinkling, magical Christmas tree; the great, poetic words of the prophet Isaiah; the careful descriptions from St Luke; and the sense of transcendence that's so splendidly rare and so utterly welcome once a year. There is *nothing* like it.

And then I realized – just when it was too late to keep moving politely on – that I'd sat in a row with a couple who had a tiny baby parked beside them. I was wedged in. No going back. This was not good.

My instant prayers fell on deaf ears. The child awoke during "Once in Royal David's City" (though mercifully *after* the choirboy had sung his mesmerizing solo lines, "Where a mother laid her baby, in a manger for his bed"). It snuffled loudly during those serene words from "Of the Father's Heart Begotten", "And the Babe, the world's Redeemer, In her loving arms received".

It burped and broke wind (I kid you not) through the reading from Isaiah 9: "For unto us a child is born..." And then it fed loudly from the breast during "Lux Aurumque" – "and the angels sing softly to the new-born babe".

Well-groomed faces began turning, to register their kindly disapproval, some time around "Hush! My dear, lie still and slumber..." And my face *may* have been among them. Finally, our row began emptying during John Tavener's sublime rendering of the Orthodox Great Compline of Christmas, as the choir gathered round the tree to conjure unspeakably beautiful harmonies from out of the ether, and the punters lost patience. "For unto us a Son is given... and his name will be called Wonderful! Counsellor!"

... And then I realized.

This whole, exquisite cathedral ritual was *about* a baby, just like the one gurgling restlessly next to me, making a nuisance of himself. The baby Jesus is like a carefully aimed spanner, thrown into the well-oiled machinery of life-as-we-know-it (religion included). And his presence continues positively to unsettle us. For the final few minutes, a soulful space opened before me in that cavernous building. The baby's eyes sparkled in the tree lights, almost knowingly.

"Veiled in flesh, the Godhead see," we sang.

I saw. Or glimpsed, at least. The baby smiled (though maybe it was wind).

"Hail, the Incarnate Deity."

Less is more? Let it snow.

Brian Draper

The author can be contacted through his website, http://www.spiritualintelligence.co.uk

Less is More Manifesto:

I will notice the way my ego pushes me, and the world of "more, bigger, faster" pulls me, in a direction that is not helpful. I will begin to notice the "call and response" below the surface of my life, between soul and Spirit, and try to let it guide me more.

I will stop buying things for the sake of it, and look instead for where the best things in life are free at the point of need. In the meantime, I will examine the things that I call "my" own, and will start to give things away, at a pace I can sustain. I will improve my quality of life without trying to buy it.

I will grow a sunflower, to remind me of the simple wisdom that will flow, if I let it, from deep within.

At the start of each day, I will remember this: I have breath, I have life, I have shelter, I am here. I will ask myself what can go right. At the end of each day, I will ask what did go right, and be thankful for it. I will focus less on the gap between me and my "competitors" and instead work on honing my own unique gift. And instead of looking jealously at others, I will encourage them to make use of their own gifts.

I will spend a manageable period of quiet during each day, when I will do nothing but listen to the silence. I will learn to befriend the silence and explore the present. I will stop wishing my life away, and settle in more fully to the unfolding rhythms of each day. I will learn from the past, and set goals for the future, but will go one purposeful step at a time, from *now* on.

I will de-clutter my mental space, keep fewer records of wrong, and spend more time letting the light into my mind from inspiring sources. I will practise contemplating "ordinary" objects, to slow myself down and sharpen my focus within the present moment.

I will look for gateways into the world of less is more, and I will deliberately step through them. I will practice lingering longer in soulful spaces, so that I can take this "spaciousness" back into the busyness of my everyday life, and let its quality be transformed.

I will learn to say more by using fewer words. And, in the meantime, I will listen more carefully to others. I will fill less diary time in advance, and think in advance about the seemingly insignificant moments of each day that I would like to regain.

I will try to do more with less. I will notice the way I oscillate between spending and renewing energy, and keep a close eye on how long I spend in the performance, renewal, survival, and burnout zones. I will create small rituals to help me flow between performance and renewal, and create positive habits within the course of each day to help me recharge as I go.

I will search for the Source of my spiritual energy, and when I find it, I will find a way of returning to it and drawing from it every day.

I will take my shoes off, every now and again, to feel the earth beneath my feet. I will do this as a simple act of reconnection. And I will let it remind me to tread lightly; to assess my carbon footprint, to consider the mark I leave as I go, and to walk more gently along the path that leads home.

I will write a six-word memoir and learn from what it says about me. Meanwhile, I will ask others to tell me their stories. I will reconsider how I define myself and others, and I will look out for how I let myself become defined.

I will stop trying to change the world,
and instead I will try to change the
world around me, by finding one thing
I would love to do, and doing it —
locally. It may not be spectacular, but
it will touch at least one other soul.
As I go, I will reflect on how, like
the kingfisher, I can be me, doing the
thing for which I came. And I will look
out for flowers on the concrete pavement
of my life.

I will try living poetically — gesture
by gesture — and see where it takes me.
I will pose less, and return instead to
a state of inner poise which will help
to shape the way I live — its form —
from the inside out.

I will stop being so judgmental of
others, especially of their outward
appearance. Each time I meet someone
new, I will try to remember that he
or she has nothing I need and act
accordingly. I will try to see the
beauty of the statue within the rough-
hewn blocks around me, and I will allow
the Sculptor of life to chip away at my
own rough edges.

I will check with myself and recheck
— which path am I walking? Which way
am I travelling? Is it towards "more,

bigger, faster" — directed by the often skewed compass of my mind — or towards the centre of life, guided by the nudge of soul and the call of the Spirit?

I will volunteer for freedom by breaking out of the norm, trying small acts of creative subversion, and remembering that I am free to choose how I respond to every situation I face. And I will dare to fail more frequently in pursuit of a life well lived.

I will choose which battles to fight, and channel my deep impulse to enter the fray on the side of what is right; on the side of the Spirit of life. And I will fight like a warrior, with creativity, in the name of love.

I will stop to listen to buskers, as a simple reminder that there is always more to this world than meets the eye. I will practise using my senses, to become more fully aware of what I'm still missing. I will get outdoors more often, and engage with the "outside world" at a visceral level. And I will learn to sense the divine presence of the Spirit, wherever I find myself.

I will allow the simplest, most powerful signs to draw me closer to the heart of

Life, to that which I may call home.
I'll let the colours of the trees remind
me, each autumn, that we have to let
go, in the end, to let come. And I will
begin, today, the process of dying, so
that I can come alive. So that I may be
born again.

I will leave the nest. I will set out.
I will trust my instinct. I will fly.

Works Mentioned in the Text

Maya Angelou, "Caged Bird", in *The Complete Collected Poems*, New York: Random House, 1994.

Neil Ansell, *Deep Country: Five Years in the Welsh Hills*, London: Penguin, 2011.

Richard Benson, "The Sensuality of the Countryside", in Bill Bryson (ed.), *Icons of England*, London: Black Swan, 2010.

Andrew Bienkowski and Mary Akers, *One Life to Give: A Path to Finding Yourself by Helping Others*, New York: The Experiment, 2010.

Paulo Coelho, *Like the Flowing River: Thoughts and Reflections*, London: Harper, 2007.

David Cooperrider, Diana Whitney, and Jacqueline M. Stavros, *Appreciative Inquiry Handbook: For Leaders of Change*, Brunswick, OH: Crown Custom Publishing, 2008.

Tim Dee, *The Running Sky: A Birdwatching Life*, London: Vintage, 2010.

John Eldredge, *Epic: The Story God is Telling*, Nashville: Thomas Nelson, 2004.

Matthew Fox, *The Hidden Spirituality of Men: Ten Metaphors to Awaken the Sacred Masculine*, Novato, CA: New World Library, 2009.

Victor Frankl, *Man's Search for Meaning*, Boston: Beacon Press, 2006.

Kahil Gilbran, *The Prophet*, London: Oneworld Publications, 1998.

Gerard Manley Hopkins, "God's Grandeur" and "As Kingfishers Catch Fire", in *Poems and Prose*, London: Penguin Classics, 1985.

Sara Maitland, *A Book of Silence*, London: Granta, 2010.

Michael McCarthy, "Mere Science Cannot Account for Beauty", *The Independent* (25 March 2011).

Christopher McDougall, *Born to Run: A Hidden Tribe, Superathletes, and the Greatest Race the World*, London: Profile Books, 2009.

The National Trust, *Simple Pleasures: Little Things That Make Life Worth Living*, London: Random House, 2010.

Ben Okri, *A Time for New Dreams*, London: Rider, 2011.

Mary Oliver, *A Poetry Handbook*, Orlando: Harcourt, 1994.

Bill Plotkin, *Soulcraft: Crossing Into the Mysteries of Nature and Psyche*, Novato, CA: New World Library, 2003.

Richard Rohr, *Falling Upward: A Spirituality for the Two Halves of Life*, San Francisco: Jossy Bass, 2011.

Tony Schwartz, *The Way We're Working Isn't Working: The Four Forgotten Needs That Energize Great Performance*, London: Simon and Schuster, 2010.

Adam Sherwin, "The Secret of Adele's Success? No Festivals, Tweeting – Or Selling Out", *The Independent* (24 May 2011).

Jamie Smyth, "Former Violent Extremists Sign up for Dublin Summit", *The Irish Times* (21 March 2011).

Eckhart Tolle, *A New Earth: Awakening to Your Life's Purpose*, New York: Dutton, 2005.

Eckhart Tolle, *The Power of Now: A Guide to Spiritual Enlightenment*, Vancouver: Namaste, 1997.

Gene Weingarten, "Pearls Before Breakfast", *The Washington Post* (8 April 2007).

Also by Brian Draper...

Spiritual Intelligence

According to the author, Danah Zohar, we live in a "spiritually dumb" culture – alienated from each other, too busy to take time to reflect, and trying desperately to juggle the myriad pulls and pushes of life without cracking up. How can we find meaning within the madness, hope within the hopelessness, reconciliation within ourselves and with our neighbour? In this book, Brian Draper asks how ordinary people, whether religious or not, can live on a daily basis with increasing wholeness and well-being – by using their spiritual intelligence.

First, we must "awaken" to new possibilities so we can "see the world afresh". Next, we "live the change", before we can finally "pass it on". Brian Draper's unique "iconic" journey of transformation – through four stages, and four levels of depth will help you to find yourself with a whole, new way of being.

"This book is inspiring."
Douglas Coupland, novelist

"Truly inspiring... a wake-up call for us all."
Oliver James, psychologist and bestselling author
of *Affluenza*

"A gem: packed full of practical suggestions which readers will find hard to ignore and written in a down-to-earth style."
The Bookseller

"I sat in a coffee shop with Brian Draper's *Spiritual Intelligence* – despite noise, I was totally absorbed. It is 'spiritual' and 'intelligent' – my mind has been illuminated and my heart warmed."
J. John, author and speaker

"It is a work of art to make a book of this nature so accessible and so understandable... people are asking themselves many questions that they may have never thought of before. This book quite rightly won't give them the answers, but will surely help them to find their own."
Sir John Whitmore, Executive Chairman, Performance Consultants International

"This is spirituality for those who want reality and depth at a time when there is so often neither. This book will transform lives, infusing the ordinary with the extraordinary, the mundane with the sacred."
Dr Mark Stibbe, Father's House Trust

"Brian Draper's beautifully written book invites us to join an exhilarating journey of discovery... It also accompanies us on the way with inspiration and practical advice. It's not *about* spiritual intelligence but a means for us to *develop* it. Read it and be transformed!"
Peter S. Heslam, Transforming Business, University of Cambridge

ISBN 978 0 7459 5321 2 | £7.99; $14.95 | Also available in digital formats

Printed in Great Britain
by Amazon.co.uk, Ltd.,
Marston Gate.